T0239404

Speed Metrics Guide

Choosing the Right Metrics to Use When Evaluating Websites

Matthew Edgar

Apress®

Speed Metrics Guide: Choosing the Right Metrics to Use When Evaluating Websites

Matthew Edgar
Centennial, CO, USA

ISBN-13 (pbk): 979-8-8688-0154-9   ISBN-13 (electronic): 979-8-8688-0155-6
https://doi.org/10.1007/979-8-8688-0155-6

Managing Director, Apress Media LLC: Welmoed Spahr
Acquisitions Editor: Shivangi Ramachandran
Development Editor: James Markham
Editorial Assistant: Jessica Vakili

Cover designed by eStudioCalamar

Distributed to the book trade worldwide by Springer Science+Business Media New York, 1 New York Plaza, Suite 4600, New York, NY 10004-1562, USA. Phone 1-800-SPRINGER, fax (201) 348-4505, e-mail orders-ny@springer-sbm.com, or visit www.springeronline.com. Apress Media, LLC is a California LLC and the sole member (owner) is Springer Science + Business Media Finance Inc (SSBM Finance Inc). SSBM Finance Inc is a **Delaware** corporation.

For information on translations, please e-mail booktranslations@springernature.com; for reprint, paperback, or audio rights, please e-mail bookpermissions@springernature.com.

Apress titles may be purchased in bulk for academic, corporate, or promotional use. eBook versions and licenses are also available for most titles. For more information, reference our Print and eBook Bulk Sales web page at http://www.apress.com/bulk-sales.

Any source code or other supplementary material referenced by the author in this book is available to readers on GitHub. For more detailed information, please visit https://www.apress.com/gp/services/source-code.

Paper in this product is recyclable

Table of Contents

About the Author

Matthew Edgar is a partner at Elementive (`www.elementive.com`), a Colorado-based consulting firm specializing in technical SEO. Over the last 20 years, Matthew has helped hundreds of clients optimize their websites, improving organic traffic and conversions. His clients include startups, small businesses, and Fortune 500 companies. Matthew is the author of *Tech SEO Guide* (Apress, 2023) and has spoken at leading SEO conferences, including SMX, MozCon, and MarTech. Matthew holds a Master's in Information and Communications Technology from the University of Denver. Learn more and connect at MatthewEdgar.net.

Introduction

The Challenge of Measuring Website Speed

The benefits of faster websites are well known. Faster websites offer a better user experience and typically have higher conversion rates. Faster websites may rank better in organic search results and are easier for robots to crawl. Because of these benefits, many companies invest heavily to improve their website's speed.

Unfortunately, companies often invest in the wrong areas and do not meaningfully improve the website's speed. Investing in the right areas and making a meaningful difference starts by understanding how to correctly measure a website's speed and knowing how to use those measurements to identify the biggest opportunities.

Speed reports can be difficult to understand with so many metrics available. TTFB, FCP, LCP, TBT, or TTI might be slow, but what do these acronyms represent about website speed? The harder question to answer is what actions should be taken if a metric is slower than it ought to be? If multiple metrics are slower than they ought to be, which metric should be improved first to have the greatest impact? Answering these questions requires not only understanding what the metric represents but also understanding how each metric relates to the bigger picture of website loading.

Understanding Speed Metrics

This book explores the different speed metrics and explains how to use each metric to evaluate the different factors contributing to slower website speeds.

There is a metric to describe each stage of a website's loading process. By using a combination of these metrics, it becomes clear which stage is slower and where investments ought to be made. This book starts at the beginning of the loading process, with metrics describing the initial connection to the website, and continues through to the end of the loading process, with metrics describing how quickly visitors can interact with the webpage.

Every chapter reviews a different metric, discussing what it measures and what it means if that metric is slow. Each chapter will also discuss ways to improve that metric. However, this is not a detailed technical discussion of how to rework the website's code or server configuration. Instead, each chapter provides an overview of related optimization tactics and summarizes the key points to consider that are most relevant to a specific metric.

Help Everyone Involved Measure Website Speed

Improving a website's speed is the responsibility of everyone working on a website. That includes the developers and engineers building the website, but also includes designers and the UX team, copywriters and content producers, marketers and SEOs, along with the company's executives. This book is written for this broader audience with the goal of helping everyone involved with the website know how to measure and evaluate a website's speed. While this book assumes readers have some general knowledge about websites, it does not assume everybody reading has a deeply technical background.

Each chapter will discuss the different tools that can be used to measure that metric and identify related opportunities for improvement. The tools discussed in this book are all available for free and can be used by everyone, including developers and non-developers. There are paid versions of these tools available that offer deeper insight, especially at scale for larger websites. While the paid versions are helpful, paying for a tool should not be a requirement. The free versions of tools offer plenty of information to begin measuring website speed and identifying opportunities.

When to Use Each Metric

Each chapter also discusses when each metric is most useful. Some metrics should be regularly monitored. Evaluating those metrics weekly, monthly, quarterly, or after major site changes can help identify opportunities and problems. Other metrics should be used during a deeper diagnostic project to investigate those opportunities and problems further. Some metrics are better to use as KPIs and include in reports for stakeholders.

Using the metrics where they are the most useful will make it easier for everyone working on the website to understand the website's speed. More importantly, with each metric used in the appropriate ways, it will be easier to determine how to make the website load faster.

PART I

Initial Connection

CHAPTER 1

DNS Lookup Time

When a visitor requests a webpage, the first step the browser takes is translating the website's domain name into an IP address. A browser needs an IP address to establish a connection with a website. For example, the domain name matthewedgar.com would be translated into the IP address 15.197.142.173. The browser retrieves the IP address from the DNS (Domain Name System) records. Because this is the first step, more time spent translating the domain into an IP address can slow subsequent steps, making the visitor wait longer to see the webpage.

What DNS Lookup Time Measures

DNS Lookup Time measures how long it takes the browser to retrieve the requested domain's IP address.

DNS Resolution Steps

The process of translating a domain name into an IP address is known as DNS resolution. The common analogy is to compare DNS resolution to looking up a person's name in a phone book to find their phone number. That analogy is helpful but oversimplifies the process of DNS resolution and leaves it unclear why DNS lookup times contribute to slower speeds. To understand the speed implications of DNS resolution, it is important to understand more details about the steps involved when a browser requests

M. Edgar, *Speed Metrics Guide*, https://doi.org/10.1007/979-8-8688-0155-6_1

the domain's IP address. These steps are shown in Figure 1-1 and include the following:

1. **Check local cache on the visitor's device:** The browser first checks if the IP address for the requested domain is cached (or saved) locally on the visitor's device. The IP address will be cached if this visitor previously visited the domain. If the IP address is found in the local cache, the browser uses that IP address to access the website and no further steps are required.

2. **DNS resolver:** If the IP address is not cached on the visitor's device, the browser sends a query to the DNS resolver to find the IP address. DNS resolvers are typically kept with the visitor's Internet Service Provider (ISP). If the IP address for a domain is already cached by the DNS resolver, the IP address is returned directly to the visitor's device. The IP address may be cached because other visitors using the same ISP have previously requested the IP address for this domain. If the IP address is not in the cache, the resolver will process the subsequent queries for the IP address. Once the IP address is returned from a query, the resolver then sends the IP address back to the visitor's device.

3. **Root server:** If the IP address was not cached by the resolver, the query is next sent to the Root DNS server. Root DNS servers store information about top-level domains (TLDs). In the URL matthewedgar.com, the TLD is .com. The Root DNS server does not contain information about

each domain's IP address. Instead, when queried, the root DNS server returns information about the location of the server that manages that TLD.

4. **TLD server:** The query for the IP address is then sent to the TLD server. This is the server responsible for managing a specific TLD, like .com. The TLD server responds with the location of the authoritative DNS server.

5. **Authoritative DNS server:** The query is next sent to the authoritative DNS server. This is the server that hosts the website or the server that manages the DNS for the domain. The authoritative DNS server looks up the IP address in its database and sends that IP address back to the browser.

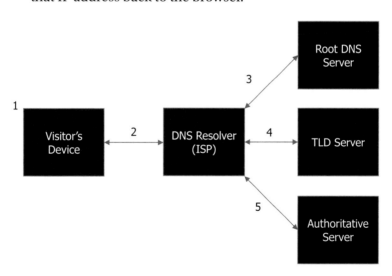

Figure 1-1. *DNS lookup process, numbers reference steps discussed in the text*

How a Visitor's Geographic Location Affects DNS Lookup Time

The servers involved in DNS resolution have a specific geographic location. The farther away the visitor's computer is physically from those servers, the longer it will take for the browser's request for the IP address to travel from the visitor's computer to the authoritative DNS server and the longer it will take for the IP address to be sent back from the authoritative DNS server to the browser. The greater the physical distance, the greater the delay, or latency, will be. Steps can be taken to minimize latency and will be discussed later in the chapter. It is important to measure DNS lookup times from anywhere in the world visitors are physically located. If most visitors are physically close to the authoritative server, then DNS lookup times will generally be faster.

DNS TTL: IP Address Cache Duration

Caching speeds up the DNS resolution process by eliminating the need to always route the query to the authoritative DNS server. However, the IP address for a domain may eventually change so it can only be saved for so long. How long the IP address can be saved in cache is specified in a DNS record's Time to Live (TTL) value. The TTL value is specified in seconds and can range from 1 second to 604,800 seconds (7 days). More typically, TTL values will be set between 30 seconds and 86,400 seconds (1 day).

Optimal DNS TTL Value

A larger TTL value will result in longer caching times. Because longer caching times reduce the steps required to retrieve an IP address, longer caching times can improve the website's speed. For example, if a visitor returns to a website within the cache time, the DNS information would not be retrieved again because that information would already be saved in the browser. Even if a particular visitor does not have the IP address information stored in the local cache, the IP address information may be cached by the visitor's ISP, eliminating the need to connect to the Root, TLD, and authoritative DNS servers.

While longer caching times may improve speed, larger TTL values also mean it takes longer to send updates to the DNS information back to a visitor. There may be an emergency, such as a server failure, that requires changing the server's IP address more quickly. If a website's TTL value is 86,400 seconds (1 day), then it would take one full day for the cache to clear and the new IP address information to be requested. Having visitors wait one full day before seeing the new IP address would not be acceptable, especially if the IP address is changed in response to an emergency.

There is not a correct TTL value. Recommendations range widely with some recommendations to set TTL values to an hour (3600 seconds) and other recommendations to set TTL values to five minutes (600 seconds) or less. Instead, the goal is to strike a balance between faster speeds and the need to respond to emergencies. If DNS lookup time is excessively long, then adjusting TTL values to increase caching times may help improve website speed.

Implications of Third-party Resources

When a website is loading, files can be requested from multiple domains. Other resources – like fonts, videos, or images – might be hosted on other domains. For example, myexamplewebsite.com might use fonts from Google's font library. If so, a DNS lookup would need to be made of fonts. gstatic.com, where the fonts are hosted along with the DNS lookup for the primary domain of myexamplewebsite.com. Each additional domain requested adds to thc total DNS lookup time.

Measuring DNS Lookup Time

DNS Lookup Time should be measured at the domain level for the primary domain and all third-party domains used by the website. Testing a single page from the domain is sufficient because this metric will not change for individual pages on the same domain. Subdomains should be tested separately if they use a separate hosting environment. For example, mysite.com may be hosted separately from images.mysite.com, each with a distinct authoritative DNS server. The DNS Lookup Time for each domain should be measured across different the different geographic locations to evaluate latency. When DNS Lookup Time is slower for a specific domain, more details about the DNS lookup process can be evaluated to determine where in the process problems might exist.

DNS Lookup Time Benchmarks

The most common recommendation comes from Sematext, which recommends DNS lookup times be between 20 and 120 milliseconds.[1] DNSPerf's benchmark test (discussed later in this section) considers DNS lookup times greater than 40 milliseconds to be slower.

Global DNS Lookup Time: DNS Speed Benchmark

DNSPerf's DNS Speed Benchmark (`www.dnsperf.com/dns-speed-benchmark`) provides a straightforward visual report that measures DNS lookup times across the world. This provides a helpful, initial review to identify what issues may exist with latency resulting from the visitor's physical location. If issues are found, then a deeper analysis can be conducted with other tools.

---

[1] "What Is DNS Lookup Time & How to Reduce It?" 2023. Sematext. September 10, 2023. `https://sematext.com/glossary/dns-lookup-time`

In DNSPerf, begin by entering the domain name to test and select the test location. By default, this tool will test DNS lookup time across the world. This could be narrowed to a continent or a country close to where visitors to this website are located. If most visitors are from the United Kingdom, latency from the United States is irrelevant.

An example result from this test is shown in Figure 1-2. Below the map, a table shows the detailed latency for specific cities, shown in Figure 1-3. In this example, the latency times are within acceptable ranges in the eastern part of the United States, with latency times well under 50 milliseconds. However, latency times worsen toward the western United States, reaching up to 84 milliseconds in Seattle. Times grow even slower outside the United States, with locations in Europe exceeding 100 milliseconds and approaching 200 milliseconds. If this website only targets visitors in the eastern United States, the DNS lookup times are acceptable. However, if this website targets visitors located elsewhere, then longer DNS lookup times would cause slower speeds.

Figure 1-2. *DNSPerf.com – DNS Speed Benchmark – map view*

LATENCY TIME ↑	LOCATION ↓		LATENCY TIME	LOCATION
224 ms	Australia, Melbourne (DC236)		211 ms	New Zealand, Auckland (DC294)
243 ms	Australia, Sydney (DC157)		140 ms	Romania, Bucharest (DC23)
280 ms	Australia, Sydney (DC264)		151 ms	Russia, Moscow (DC271)
196 ms	Australia, Sydney (DC371)		152 ms	Russia, Saint Petersburg (DC38)
136 ms	Austria, Vienna (DC154)		123 ms	Slovakia, Bratislava (DC104)
96 ms	Brazil, Salvador (DC470)		248 ms	South Africa, Cape Town (DC526)
111 ms	Brazil, Sao Paulo (DC436)		271 ms	South Africa, Johannesburg (DC317)
116 ms	Brazil, Sao Paulo (DC269)		164 ms	Turkey, Bursa (DC161)
116 ms	Brazil, Sao Paulo (DC393)		156 ms	Turkey, Istanbul (DC513)
Record Not Found	China, Beijing (DC207)		99 ms	United Kingdom, London (DC346)
147 ms	Egypt, Cairo (DC464)		100 ms	United Kingdom, London (DC61)
143 ms	Finland, Helsinki (DC228)		28 ms	United States, Ashburn (DC378)
112 ms	France, Marseille (DC525)		31 ms	United States, Chicago (DC339)
111 ms	Germany, Frankfurt am Main (DC426)		56 ms	United States, Denver (DC428)

Figure 1-3. *DNSPerf.com DNS Speed Benchmark test – detailed table of latency by location*

Domain Connections: WebPageTest

Third-party resources hosted on other domains require separate DNS connections, adding to the overall load time for the website. To determine if third-party resources are contributing to slower speeds, DNS lookup times should be measured for all third-party domains used on the website. If DNS lookup times are slower for certain domains, using *prefetch* (discussed later in this chapter) may help.

WebPageTest (`www.webpagetest.org/`) measures the DNS lookup times for the website's primary domain and any third-party domains used by the website. WebPageTest tests can be run from different locations, helping to show variance due to geographic latency. WebPageTest provides a few locations on the "Simple Configuration" settings, while the "Advanced Configuration" settings provide a wider list of test locations. These tests should be run on different pages of the website as each page may use different third-party resources.

Information about third-party resources is provided in the "Connection View" report. After running a test on WebPageTest, access this report by selecting "Details" in the "View" menu and then scroll to "Connection View." As seen in the example "Connection View" report, shown in Figure 1-4, each domain requested when loading this page on the website is listed. Looking horizontally across the chart, a bar is provided for each domain showing different aspects of that domain's loading process. DNS lookup times are in the first part of that bar, indicated by the arrow providing a visual of how much time DNS resolution consumes for the primary domain and every third-party domain used on the tested page.

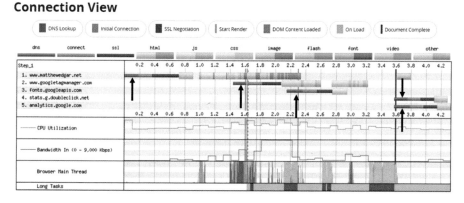

Figure 1-4. *WebPageTest – Connection View report showing the load times for each domain*

Specific DNS lookup times, shown in milliseconds, can be measured using the "Request Details" table below the "Connection View" report, shown in Figure 1-5. Sort the table by the "DNS Lookup" column to see the milliseconds required to connect to that domain.

Request Details

| Before Start Render | Before On Load | After On Load | 3xx Response | 4xx Response |

Request Details

#	Resource	Content Type	Priority	Request Start	DNS Lookup	Initial Connection	SSL Negotiation	Time to First Byte	Content Download	Bytes Downloaded	CPU Time
32	https://analytics.go...for_viewport=360x512	text/plain	Lowest	4.111 s	209 ms	172 ms	192 ms	183 ms	-	-	-
1	https://www.matthewedgar.net/	text/html	Highest	0.746 s	208 ms	173 ms	363 ms	184 ms	1 ms	6.6 KB	15 ms
28	https://fonts.google...00.900&display=swap	text/css	High	2.712 s	178 ms	172 ms	184 ms	190 ms	2 ms	0.8 KB	-
27	https://www.googleta...gtm.js?id=GTM-KTC8NN	application/javascript	Low	2.071 s	173 ms	178 ms	276 ms	256 ms	258 ms	50.4 KB	138 m
31	https://stats.g.doub...6>m=45je37g0&aip=1	text/plain	Lowest	4.097 s	172 ms	186 ms	197 ms	201 ms	-	-	-

Figure 1-5. *WebPageTest – Request Details table showing the DNS Lookup time for each domain used by this webpage*

Dig Test: DiG GUI

Domain Information Groper (dig) tests provide more details about the query and response process. Dig tests are useful when a deeper diagnosis is needed because tools like DNSPerf or WebPageTest show slower DNS lookup times.

While dig tests can be run on a local computer, it is easier to use an online tool, such as DiG GUI (`www.diggui.com/`). On DiG GUI, enter the website URL in the hostname field. Example test results are shown in Figure 1-6. The answer section shows the IP address for this domain and the DNS's TTL values. In the example shown, TTL is 21600 seconds or 6 hours. Below the answer section, the results show the query time, which in this example is 19 milliseconds.

```
; <<>> DiG diggui.com <<>> @8.8.8.8 matthewedgar.net A
; (1 server found)
;; global options: +cmd
;; Got answer:
;; ->>HEADER<<- opcode: QUERY, status: NOERROR, id: 60550
;; flags: qr rd ra; QUERY: 1, ANSWER: 1, AUTHORITY: 0, ADDITIONAL: 1

;; OPT PSEUDOSECTION:
; EDNS: version: 0, flags:; udp: 512
;; QUESTION SECTION:
;matthewedgar.net.              IN      A

;; ANSWER SECTION:
matthewedgar.net.       21600   IN      A       35.212.66.223

;; Query time: 19 msec
;; SERVER: 8.8.8.8#53(8.8.8.8)
```

Figure 1-6. *Dig test results from diggui.com*

DiG GUI provides additional options to further investigate DNS lookup times. One of the more helpful options is trace, which shows more details about the step-by-step DNS query process. This can help with further diagnosis of any issues that may exist.

Ways to Improve DNS Lookup Time

Improving DNS latency often requires significant and complex changes, including enhancing network connectivity and adjusting the way DNS is managed. More significant improvements typically require bigger investments because they require support from highly specialized professionals. However, there are simpler, less complex methods to consider first to improve slower DNS lookup times.

Select Faster DNS Provider

One of the most effective and simplest ways to reduce DNS lookup times is to use a different DNS provider that can return the IP address to the browser more quickly. The DNS provider manages the DNS records for a domain.

Many companies choose a default option, allowing the domain registrar or website hosting company to manage the domain's DNS. This can lead to acceptable performance if the registrar or hosting company manages DNS quickly. However, the registrar or hosting company might not manage DNS as effectively as a dedicated DNS provider. Switching to a dedicated DNS provider could reduce DNS lookup times.

Dedicated DNS providers achieve faster speeds because they have more infrastructure available to respond to DNS queries and that infrastructure is better distributed globally, allowing DNS providers to reduce latency. DNSPerf's "DNS Providers List" reports on the DNS lookup times for various providers (`www.dnsperf.com/dns-providers-list`). An example is shown in Figure 1-7. For example, Cloudflare has a query time of 12.41 milliseconds and is one of the fastest providers because it uses a global server distribution that places servers physically closer to the person visiting the website and reduces latency.

DNS Providers list

DNS providers sorted by DNSPerf rank ⓘ based on data for last 30 days

DNSPerf rank ↕	DNS Provider ↕		Uptime ↕	Quality ↕	Query time ↕
1	CLOUDFLARE	Cloudflare	99.96%	99.94%	12.41 ms
2	SECTIGO®	Sectigo Premium	99.97%	99.94%	14.86 ms
3	Edgio	Edgio	99.98%	99.94%	16.13 ms
6	WORDPRESS	WordPress.com	99.95%	99.88%	18.85 ms
7	DNS MADE EASY	DNSMadeEasy by DigiCert	99.96%	99.89%	19.66 ms

Figure 1-7. DNS Providers list from DNSPerf – www.dnsperf.com/dns-providers-list

Prefetch Third-Party Domains: *dns-prefetch* and *preconnect*

Connecting to third-party domains contributes to total DNS lookup times. This can be improved by removing unneeded third-party resources. However, not all third-party resources can be removed. For those that cannot be removed, a *dns-prefetch* link tag can be added to the <head> section of a webpage's HTML code. This tag instructs the browser to fetch DNS information for the specified domain earlier in the loading process.

For example, if the following code were added to the webpage's <head>, the browser would perform the DNS lookup for the third-party domain otherdomain.com earlier in the website loading process and cache that DNS information locally. When the browser later requests a file from otherdomain.com – such as an image, video, or font – the IP address for this domain will already be saved in the cache.

```
<link rel="dns-prefetch" href="https://www.otherdomain.com/" />
```

15

This tag should only be used for cross-origin domains, not the primary domain. The website myexamplewebsite.com would never need to use a *dns-prefetch* for myexamplewebsite.com. The browser has already made a connection to the primary domain by the time the browser would see the *dns-prefetch* link tag in the webpage's HTML code.

A connection can also be made with the *preconnect* link tag. A *preconnect* requests DNS information along with establishing a TCP and TLS connection to that server. TCP and TLS connections will be discussed in more detail in the next chapter. Like *dns-prefetch*, when a browser encounters *preconnect*, it will complete the DNS request, the TCP connection, and the TLS connection earlier in the process to prepare that domain for later use. This can improve how quickly the browser is able to load files from third-party domains. However, the *preconnect* tag requires the browser to do more work than *dns-prefetch*, so *preconnect* can slow speeds if it is not used correctly. Typically, a *preconnect* should only be used for the most critical resources and a *dns-prefetch* for less critical third-party resources. This will be discussed more in Chapter 5. An example *preconnect* tag is shown in the following. Like with the *dns-prefetch* tag, the *preconnect* tag is placed in the webpage's HTML <head> section.

```
<link rel="preconnect" href="https://www.otherdomain.com/" />
```

Recap: When to Use DNS Lookup Time

DNS Lookup Time is most helpful as a diagnostic metric to understand the very first step a web browser takes to connect to a website.

- **Is the reporting scope meaningful?** DNS lookup times measure one specific action – an important action, but still only one single action the browser takes to load a website. Because it has such a narrow scope, DNS Lookup Time is most helpful to review as part of a deeper diagnostic project investigating all aspects of a website's speed to determine if problems exist in the very first step of connecting to a website. However, it is usually too narrowly scoped to be meaningful as part of regular monitoring or regular reporting, where slightly broader metrics are typically more useful.

- **Is it an effective business goal?** Because of the narrow scope, DNS lookup times do not directly relate to business goals, like conversions and engagement. Slower DNS lookup times may indirectly affect business goals because of the slower initial connection to the website. This indirect connection to business goals makes it an unhelpful speed KPI to share with a broader group of stakeholders. Also, many companies do not always have control over DNS lookups so even if DNS Lookup Time is slow, it is less actionable than other metrics.

- **Does it describe the user experience?** As an early-stage metric, slower DNS lookup times can slow other later-stage metrics and, by doing so, slow the website for visitors. However, DNS lookup times do not describe the specific experience visitors have on the website. Also, there are still ways to deliver a satisfyingly fast experience for visitors even with a slower DNS Lookup Time by improving later-stage metrics.

- **How easy is it to improve?** While changing the DNS provider or changing how third-party resources are loaded can reduce DNS lookup times, more extensive and highly technical changes are needed if those steps are insufficient. This can make it challenging to fully optimize DNS lookup times. Also, there are limited options to improve third-party resources and removing third-party resources is not always an option if those resources are critical for the overall operation of a website.

- **How impactful are improvements?** If DNS lookups are contributing to slower load times, improvements can be very impactful. Because DNS lookup time measures the very first step taken to load a website, any improvements will be reflected in later-stage metrics. This is especially true when DNS lookup times are improved in geographic locations with greater latency. However, there are minimal impacts from further improvements if DNS lookup times are already within acceptable levels.

CHAPTER 2

Time to First Byte (TTFB)

Retrieving DNS information is the first of many steps involved in loading a webpage. Next, the browser and server need to establish a connection. Once the connection is established, the browser sends the server details about the webpage visitors requested and the server starts building the necessary files to fulfill the visitor's request. As the files are prepared, the server sends the files for this webpage to the browser one byte at a time. Visitors, meanwhile, see a blank screen while the browser and server do this work.

What Time to First Byte Measures

Time to First Byte (TTFB) is the time between the browser sending the initial request for the page to the server and the server returning the first byte of data to the browser.

Process Before the Server Sends the First Byte

There are five steps (broadly speaking) that occur before the server returns the first byte of data to the browser. As shown in Figure 2-1, those five steps are:

1. **DNS lookup:** After a URL is requested, the browser needs to lookup the DNS information for the domain. This process was discussed in detail in Chapter 1. TTFB includes DNS Lookup Time.

© Matthew Edgar 2024
M. Edgar, *Speed Metrics Guide*, https://doi.org/10.1007/979-8-8688-0155-6_2

2. **TCP connection:** Once the browser has the IP address, the browser establishes a Transmission Control Protocol (TCP) connection. This connection allows for communication between the browser and the server.

3. **TSL/SSL handshake:** If the website is secured (the URL starts with https://), then the browser and server next establish how to communicate securely in a Transport Security Layer (TSL) handshake. During this step, the browser also verifies the security certificate.

4. **Server builds response:** Once communication has been established and security has been verified, the browser sends the HTTP request to the server with information about the file being requested. The server processes the necessary code to build the response for that request and, once the response is prepared, the server sends the first byte of data to the browser.

5. **Browser receives the first byte of data:** Finally, the browser receives the first byte of data. The first byte of data is the first byte of the HTTP response headers. HTTP response headers are a plain text field sent along with the page's content and contain information about the file returned. That includes information about the file's status code, the file's last modified date, or caching instructions.

Figure 2-1. Process to send first byte of data to the browser

How Servers Build a Response

Typically, the time the server spends building the request – in the preceding step 4 – is the biggest factor contributing to TTFB. To build the response, the server first receives an HTTP request from the browser with instructions on what file should be returned. The request includes the requested URL, authentication information, information about what language or encoding will be accepted in a response, and information about the user agent making the request (the user agent indicates who is making the request, such as Googlebot or a visitor using Safari on an iPhone).

Once received, the server follows those instructions to begin generating a response. The server starts by determining what files are needed to generate that response. If those files are static, like a plain HTML file or an image, the response is easier for the server to generate. The server does not need to process static files further and can send that file back to the browser as is.

However, many pages on websites are not static. Instead, dynamic files are written in a server-side programming language. The server has specific handlers installed to execute code written in that specific language. For example, WordPress is written in PHP code and a website using WordPress will be hosted on a server that can process that PHP code. When a page is requested on a WordPress website, the server needs to use PHP handlers to execute all required PHP code. The PHP code may be spread across multiple files, all of which need to be retrieved by the server before processing those files to build the response.

As part of executing the code, typically data must also be retrieved from a database. Along with executing the code, the server establishes a database connection and queries the necessary information from a database. In WordPress, for example, the page's text is saved in a MySQL database and that text needs to be retrieved from the database for the page to be fully assembled. In most cases, multiple database queries are needed to retrieve a page's information.

21

The more involved the code and the more data that needs to be queried from the database, the longer this process can take. Optimizing this process is one of the most effective ways to improve TTFB. Optimizations include simplifying code, simplifying database queries, and removing any errors in the code.

After querying the database and executing the code, the server assembles the final HTML code for the requested HTML page. In the final steps of building the response, the server also logs the request made and logs any errors that occurred during the building process. The server then generates the response headers the browser will need to process the request and then, finally, the server sends the requested file to the browser.

How Redirects Impact TTFB

Any URL that redirects will have a longer TTFB because both the URL being redirected from (the source or origin) and the URL being redirected to (the target or destination) will need to be retrieved and processed. Updating links on the website to avoid redirects is one way to reduce how much TTFB visitors experience. That way, visitors will not be forced to load redirects when clicking links on the website. However, the level of impact of the redirect and the overall importance of updating links to that redirect will differ depending on the redirect destination.

Scenario 1: Redirect Destination URL on the Same Domain

In this scenario, the redirect destination is another URL on the same domain. For example, the URL asite.com/abc redirects to asite.com/xyz. For this type of redirect, the first three steps outlined previously will only need to be completed once, but more time will be required during the fourth step for building the response. The server spends additional time identifying that the initial URL requested should redirect, finding what the redirect destination is, and then processing the redirect. The server may also need to execute additional code or query a database related to the URL that redirects. For example, the redirect instructions for a URL may be stored in a database, so the server would need to execute the required code to query the redirect from the database before being able to process the redirect.

An example of this type of redirect is shown in Figure 2-2. The URL requested in the first line redirects. The narrow bar on that first line has three distinct blocks indicating the DNS lookup time, TCP connection, and SSL handling. The thicker bar on the first line, indicated by the arrow, shows the time the server needs to process the redirect. The second line shows the redirect destination URL. On this second line, there is only the thicker bar, as the only time spent was the server processing the redirect destination URL. In the example shown in Figure 2-2, the thicker part of the bar in the first line represents the extra time added to TTFB because of the redirect.

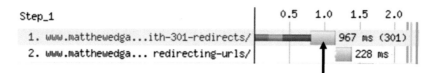

Figure 2-2. *Server-side redirect to URL on same domain. Test conducted with WebPageTest*

Scenario 2: Redirect Destination URL on Another Domain

When a redirect destination URL is located on a different domain, the first three steps will need to be repeated for both URLs. The URL that redirects and the redirect destination URL are on separate domains, therefore a separate connection will need to be made to each domain.

An example of this is shown in Figure 2-3. The first line is the same as the first line in the previous scenario. The difference is in the second line, where the DNS lookup, server connection, and SSL handling must be repeated because the redirect destination URL is on a different domain. As a result, the entire first line shows the extra time added to the TTFB because of the redirect.

Figure 2-3. *Server-side redirect to URL on a different domain. Test conducted with WebPageTest*

Implications of Third-party Resources

If the files used to load the website are hosted on different domains, the browser must follow the same steps outlined previously to connect to each individual domain and request files from those domains. For example, myexamplewebsite.com might use fonts from Google's font library. In this example, the browser would need to establish separate connections to myexamplewebsite.com and fonts.gstatic.com. The browser would need to wait to receive data from both domains before completing the page load. A third-party domain with a longer TTFB will slow the overall website load. However, even third-party domains with faster TTFB can slow website load if several third-party domains are used. TTFB should be measured for each domain used to load the website.

Measuring Time to First Byte

TTFB should be measured on a page-by-page basis. It is important to evaluate different page types because some types of pages require more processing time than others. For example, on an ecommerce website, product pages may have a slower TTFB than blog posts because the server executes more code and database queries to build product pages. TTFB can also differ depending on the visitor's geographic location, with greater distances causing greater latency. So, the TTFB for each page should be evaluated for the main countries and regions visitors are located in. If TTFB is slower, the details about the individual steps involved in the connection process can be evaluated to determine which steps are the most important to improve.

TTFB Benchmarks

Google's guidelines recommend TTFB be kept under 800 milliseconds to be considered fast and that a TTFB greater than 1800 milliseconds (1.8 seconds) will be considered slow.[1] Only 40.7% of mobile websites and only 53.5% of desktop websites have a TTFB under 800 milliseconds, according to HTTP Archive's data assessing TTFB across millions of websites.[2]

TTFB by Location: KeyCDN Performance Test

KeyCDN's Performance Test (`https://tools.keycdn.com/performance`) offers a way of measuring TTFB by location. Enter the URL for a page and then a table will load showing TTFBs for different geographic locations. An example result is shown in Figure 2-4. While this does not represent TTFB for actual visitors, the locations are spread across the world to give an indication of where problems may exist. In addition, this report shows how DNS lookup time, server connection (TCP connection), and the TLS handshake contribute to TTFB by location, helping to explain why TTFB may be higher for some visitors.

---

[1] Wagner, Jeremy, and Barry Pollard. 2021. "Time to First Byte (TTFB)." Web.dev. Google Developers. October 26, 2021. `https://web.dev/articles/ttfb`

[2] "Report: CrUX." 2023. HTTP Archive. September 1, 2023. `https://httparchive.org/reports/chrome-ux-report#cruxFastTtfb`

LOCATION	STATUS	DNS	CONNECT	TLS	TTFB	
🇩🇪 Frankfurt	200	6.65 ms	92.1 ms	208.99 ms	521.14 ms	⌄
🇳🇱 Amsterdam	200	32.52 ms	92.56 ms	191.24 ms	492.05 ms	⌄
🇬🇧 London	200	24.7 ms	81.24 ms	175.93 ms	463.4 ms	⌄
🇺🇸 New York	200	30.79 ms	9.39 ms	32.66 ms	174.91 ms	⌄
🇺🇸 San Francisco	200	23.68 ms	70.72 ms	151.25 ms	416.16 ms	⌄
🇸🇬 Singapore	200	11.52 ms	220.67 ms	451.92 ms	1.01 s	⌄
🇦🇺 Sydney	200	114.4 ms	211.71 ms	494.05 ms	1.04 s	⌄
🇮🇳 Bangalore	200	90.15 ms	240.49 ms	490.25 ms	1.11 s	⌄

Figure 2-4. *KeyCDN performance test – TTFB by location*

TTFB Details: Byte Check

If KeyCDN or other tools show a higher TTFB, the next step is to determine why TTFB is higher. Byte Check (`www.bytecheck.com/`) offers a simple but effective tool to see the speed of each step contributing to TTFB to narrow down what to fix. Byte Check also shows how redirects impact TTFB.

An example result for a redirected link is shown in Figure 2-5. In this example, the redirect time is only 36.64 milliseconds and not contributing greatly to TTFB. Instead, the largest factor contributing to TTFB on this page is the Wait time of 1417.11 milliseconds. The Wait time is how long it takes the server to process files before sending data to the browser. The page used in this example is dynamic, requiring the server to process lots of code and execute several data queries. TTFB should be addressed on this page or other similar types of pages on the website.

Figure 2-5. *Results from Byte Check showing details of TTFB process, including a redirect and a longer Wait time*

In Figure 2-6, a simpler page on the same website only has a Wait time of 36.31 milliseconds. TTFB is not a concern for this page or other pages of this type.

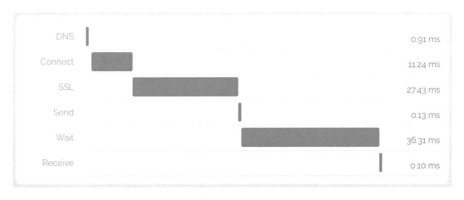

Figure 2-6. *Result from Byte Check for a simpler page, with less Wait time*

TTFB Additional Details: WebPageTest

Byte Check's data is helpful but limited to a single test location. TTFB can change for visitors in different locations or using different device types. To better understand these differences, a page's TTFB can be evaluated in WebPageTest (`www.webpagetest.org/`), which allows for tests to be run from different locations, on different device types, and at different connection speeds. A few options are provided with the default "Simple Configuration" and more options are available under WebPageTest's "Advanced Configuration" settings. Selecting the device types and locations that best represent the visitors to a website will provide the most meaningful results.

After running a test, select "Details" in the "View" menu to access the "Performance Details" report. The top of the report shows a summary of key metrics, including TTFB. The example webpage shown in Figure 2-7 has a TTFB of 340 milliseconds.

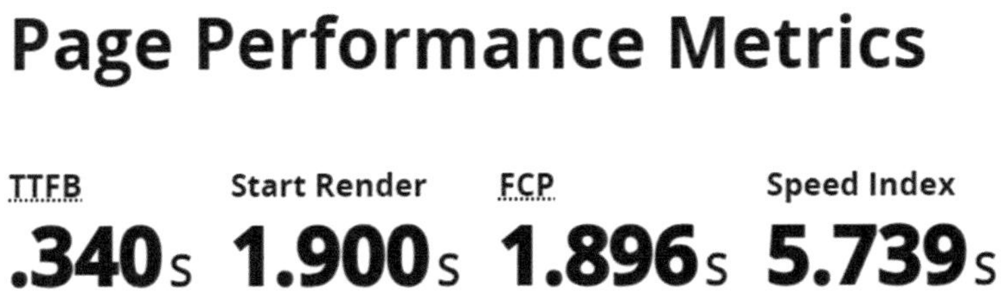

Page Performance Metrics

TTFB	Start Render	FCP	Speed Index
.340s	1.900s	1.896s	5.739s

Figure 2-7. *WebPageTest Page Performance Metrics, including TTFB*

On this same page, the "Request Details" table provides details about each request, including time for each step of TTFB. The Time to First Byte column in this table only represents the final steps of the server building the request and sending the first byte of data to the browser. In the example shown in Figure 2-8, the DNS lookup takes 87 milliseconds, connecting to the server (the TCP connection) takes 43 milliseconds, the SSL negotiation (the TSL handshake) takes 62 milliseconds, and it takes 148 milliseconds for the server to build the response and send the first byte of data to the browser. This adds up to a total TTFB of 340 milliseconds (matching the TTFB shown in Figure 2-7). The "Request Details" table will also provide these metrics for any resources from third-party domains.

				Request Details			
Resource	Content Type	Priority	Request Start	DNS Lookup	Initial Connection	SSL Negotiation	Time to First Byte
https://www.examplesite.com	text/html	Highest	0.192 s	87 ms	43 ms	62 ms	148 ms

Figure 2-8. *WebPageTest Request Details report with time for each TTFB step broken out in the DNS Lookup, Initial Connection, SSL Negotiation, and Time to First Byte columns. The Time to First Byte column only reflects the final steps of the process and not the full TTFB discussed throughout this chapter*

Ways to Improve Time to First Byte

Before optimizing TTFB, it is important to know which step contributes the most to TTFB using the tools discussed in the previous section. Each step of the process needs to be optimized with a unique set of tactics. If the DNS lookup time is slow, no amount of optimizing the backend code will help improve TTFB. Slower DNS lookup times require making changes like those discussed in Chapter 1. Slower TSL handshake times require optimizing SSL certificates and secure connections. Typically, TSL handshakes do not contribute significantly to TTFB. Most often, TTFB involves optimizing the backend of the website, including tactics like caching resources or selecting a faster hosting provider.

Caching Internal Resources

Server processing is slower when pages are more complex. For more complex pages, the server needs to execute more code and make several database queries to fully build the page. Improving TTFB requires optimizing this code and database queries as much as possible. For example, using indexes on database columns, avoiding subqueries, or using more efficient join types can help make database queries run faster.

Along with code or database changes, TTFB can also be improved by evaluating pages to see if everything presented on the page is necessary for visitors. Removing complicated features or functionality to simplify the page can improve TTFB. Removing features on a page will reduce the code the server needs to process to generate that page.

However, there are limits to how much code and database queries can be optimized and how much the page can be simplified. The next best option is to use caching. A cache is a static file that contains the results of a database query or the output of a website's backend code. While a full page can be cached, in other cases, only specific parts of the page or specific database queries are cached. When the first visitor requests a page, the server will do the work to execute the code and run the database queries. Then, the server will save the results of the code and database query to a cached file. The next time a visitor requests the same page, the server will return the contents of the cached file instead of re-running the code or database queries. Because a cached file is static, the server does less work to return that page and that is why caching can speed up TTFB for subsequent visits.

The cache needs to be refreshed after a certain time interval to prevent the cache from growing stale. The correct interval will vary depending on the page's content. The cache of a news website's homepage might need to be refreshed multiple times per hour, but a cache of a news article might only need to be refreshed daily.

Once caching is implemented, re-test cached pages to see what difference the caching has made. Byte Check makes this easier to see visually by comparing the bar lengths for Wait Time before and after caching was implemented. Caching may not fix every problem contributing to TTFB. Figure 2-5 showed a longer Wait time even though caching was enabled for that website. If Wait time is still longer after caching resources, the next step is to review the hosting provider's server configuration.

Choose Faster Hosting Provider

Even with optimization and caching, code and database queries will still run slowly if the server is poorly configured. It is important to select a faster hosting provider that can execute the code and query databases as quickly as possible. Better hosting providers will offer servers with sufficient memory capable of processing requests and greater bandwidth to increase data transfer capacity. Some hosting providers distribute servers globally, reducing latency due to the visitor's location. Also, some hosting providers have built-in caching functionality to improve speeds.

However, a faster hosting provider may not be able to load every type of website quickly. When comparing hosting companies, it is important to select a hosting company that works with the website's specific technical requirements. For example, several hosting companies provide a hosting environment optimized to efficiently run WordPress websites, but non-WordPress websites will often run more slowly in those environments.

The website IsMyHostFastYet.com compares TTFB values for real-world visitors across multiple hosting providers and can be a helpful resource to consult when comparing possible hosting providers. An example result for top hosting companies is shown in Figure 2-9.

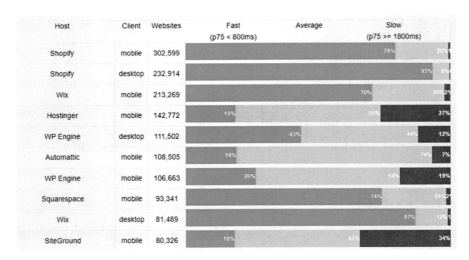

Figure 2-9. *Example result from IsMyHostFastYet.com showing TTFB distribution for websites using that host*

Recap: When to Use Time to First Byte

TTFB is best used as part of regular monitoring to understand the speed of the initial website connection and identify problems within the first stages of loading the website.

- **Is the reporting scope meaningful?** TTFB has a broader scope, measuring the entirety of the initial stages of loading a website. It encompasses times for DNS lookup, TCP connection, TSL/SSL negotiation, and server processing. Monitoring TTFB regularly will help identify any problems in these early stages. Increases in TTFB should be investigated immediately because a slow TTFB can affect other later-stage metrics. TTFB is also important to test after major redevelopment projects where server processing can change substantially. When used, it is important to remember that TTFB is only helpful to describe the initial connection but that it does not describe anything about what happens after the initial connection has been made.

- **Is it an effective business goal?** TTFB is an effective metric for those operating at a tactical level. A higher TTFB is often an underlying cause for other later-stage metrics being higher. Those operating at a strategic level will typically find TTFB less helpful because improvements in TTFB do not directly correlate to improvements in engagement, conversions, or other key business objectives. As a result, TTFB is typically best used in regular monitoring reports instead of including TTFB as a KPI in reports for a broader group of stakeholders.

- **Does it describe the user experience?** Like DNS Lookup Time discussed in Chapter 1, because TTFB is an early-stage performance indicator, any impact TTFB has on user experience will be indirect. A slower TTFB can slow subsequent steps in the website load, but a slower TTFB does not always indicate a poor experience for visitors. The initial connection might be slower, but the rest of the website could load much faster.

- **How easy is it to improve?** Most of TTFB is consumed by the server processing needed to deliver the first byte of data to the browser. This means organizations typically have a lot of control over the factors contributing to a longer TTFB. However, optimizing database queries, configuring caching, compressing files (see Chapter 4), and similar types of work are never easy, especially on more complex websites. Sometimes, the level of investment needed to improve TTFB is prohibitive, and there are less expensive options available to improve other speed metrics.

- **How impactful are improvements?** TTFB is an early-stage metric, so any improvements in TTFB often improve the later stages of the website's load. This can make TTFB improvements highly impactful. However, there can be other problems later in the website loading process that slow the website's load, negating the benefits of a faster TTFB. Before investing in TTFB improvements, which can often be substantial, it is important to evaluate how much a slow TTFB impacts the later stages of a website's load.

PART II

Displaying the Page

CHAPTER 3

DOMContentLoaded Time

After the server sends the first byte of data to the browser for the requested page, the server continues sending additional data to the browser. This includes sending the requested webpage's HTML code. The browser processes and analyzes the HTML code to determine how to construct the page. Nothing is displayed for visitors yet and the more HTML code there is for the browser to process, the longer it will take to reach the steps where visitors are able to see something.

What DOMContentLoaded Measures

DOMContentLoaded (DCL) time measures the time between the initial request for the webpage and when the browser has fully parsed the webpage's HTML to construct the **Document Object Model (DOM)**. At DCL time, stylesheets, images, and other resources have not finished loading.

HTML Parsing

As it receives the HTML code from the server, the browser analyzes and processes the HTML code to determine how to present it to the visitor. These processing and analyzing operations are called parsing. During parsing,

© Matthew Edgar 2024
M. Edgar, *Speed Metrics Guide*, https://doi.org/10.1007/979-8-8688-0155-6_3

the browser breaks the HTML into various components – individual tags, attributes within the tags, and the content (including text) contained in those tags. The browser also handles any errors found within the code when parsing. Excessive errors can slow parsing.

Once the webpage's HTML code has been loaded and parsed, the browser triggers the DOMContentLoaded (or DCL) event. The DCL time captures the entire time from the initial connection to the website up to when the DCL event is triggered. That means, DCL time includes everything measured by TTFB. It is important to remember that at DCL, other files – stylesheets, images, videos, and so on – have not finished loading.

Document Object Model (DOM)

Parsing generates the Document Object Model (DOM). The DOM is a hierarchical structure representing the webpage's HTML code. It is often visually represented as a tree, as shown in Figure 3-1. The browser uses the DOM when in the later stages of rendering and painting (discussed in Chapter 5). A larger DOM size requires more parsing, delaying rendering and painting.

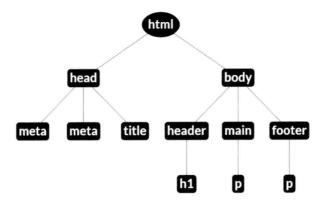

Figure 3-1. DOM Tree example – generated from `https://fritscher.ch/dom-css/`

The DOM contains elements and nodes. An element is a specific HTML tag, like <h1> (heading level 1) or <p> (paragraph). A node is a more general concept representing all components in the HTML, including all elements as well as comments, whitespace, and text. Only DOM elements are shown in Figure 3-1's example DOM tree.

How CSS Affects Parsing

During HTML parsing, the browser will encounter CSS code. CSS stands for Cascading Style Sheets and is a language that provides instructions about how to visually display the page. Typically, CSS is added with a reference to an external stylesheet. For example, this <link> tag would be found in the <head> section of an HTML page and references the main. css file.

```
<link rel="stylesheet" href="main.css" />
```

When this type of reference to an external CSS file is encountered, the browser will not pause the HTML parsing. Instead, the browser will add the external stylesheet to a loading queue and return to it once the HTML parsing is completed. The CSS will then be parsed separately. External stylesheets do not block parsing but can block other parts of displaying the page, as will be discussed in Chapter 5.

CSS can also be included via an embedded stylesheet. Embedded stylesheets add CSS code directly in the HTML document inside a <style> tag. For example, this embedded stylesheet gives any element with the class cta_button a red background and makes the button text bold.

```
<style>
.cta_button {
  background-color: red;
  font-weight: bold;
}
</style>
```

When the parser encounters the embedded stylesheet, it briefly stops parsing the HTML code to parse the CSS code. This means the embedded stylesheet can slow HTML parsing and increase DCL time, though the impacts are typically minimal unless a lot of CSS code is included. The biggest advantage of an embedded stylesheet is the browser parses this CSS code more quickly than it will parse an external stylesheet. This is because with an external stylesheet, the browser must load the additional file before it can parse the document. By parsing that CSS code more quickly, the browser has those styles available to use sooner when displaying the page. This is why some recommend an embedded stylesheet for CSS code related to the page's most critical elements.

How JavaScript Affects Parsing

During HTML parsing, the browser also encounters JavaScript in the webpage's HTML code. JavaScript is loaded synchronously by default. This means when JavaScript code is detected by the browser during parsing, the browser will pause all HTML parsing activity so that it can request and download the JavaScript file, process the JavaScript code, and then execute that code. The JavaScript code is requested, downloaded, processed, and executed in the order it is presented in the HTML document. This is true whether the JavaScript code is embedded within the HTML document or included in a separate file. When JavaScript code is embedded directly in the HTML document, no additional JavaScript file needs to be requested or downloaded.

The browser stops HTML parsing to execute JavaScript code because the JavaScript code can manipulate the DOM. JavaScript can add or remove HTML elements, alter existing HTML elements, or update the text inside HTML elements. Those types of changes could alter how the browser needs to construct the DOM. If the browser waited for HTML parsing to fully complete before executing any JavaScript code, then HTML parsing might need to happen multiple times to account for those DOM changes.

As a result, pausing parsing can help improve speed when there is JavaScript code used on the website that will manipulate the DOM. There are exceptions. If the JavaScript runs slower or an external JavaScript file takes longer to load, pausing parsing to load and execute JavaScript code can slow DCL time to an unacceptable level. JavaScript code can also expand the DOM to an unruly size that can make it harder for the browser to load the website efficiently.

Some JavaScript code does not manipulate the DOM, resulting in pauses that slow DCL time unnecessarily. For example, JavaScript code containing tracking scripts typically do not make any changes to the DOM. Other JavaScript code will only change the DOM at a later point, such as a script that loads new content when visitors interact with a certain feature. These types of scripts could be loaded later and in a way that will not slow DCL time.

The "Ways to Improve" section later in this chapter discusses the impact of deferring JavaScript files or loading JavaScript code asynchronously to help avoid unnecessary parsing delays.

Measuring DOMContentLoaded

Each page's HTML code is unique and will have different DCL times and DOM sizes. As well, the server might be configured to send different HTML code based on the visitor's device type or JavaScript code might change the HTML output based on the visitor's device type. As a result, DCL time and DOM size should be measured for a variety of pages on mobile and desktop devices. When analyzing website speed, it is typically helpful to measure DCL time and DOM size on the website's most complex pages because those will contain more HTML code for the browser to load and parse.

DCL Time Benchmarks

Unlike other metrics, there are no target guidelines for DCL time. HTTP Archive's analysis of millions of websites reports a median DCL time of 6.2 seconds on mobile devices and 3.1 seconds on desktop devices.[1] From the same data, 75% of websites had a DCL time of up to 9 seconds on mobile devices and up to 4.8 seconds on desktop devices. However, the top 10% of websites were able to load and parse the HTML within 3.1 seconds on mobile and 1.4 seconds on desktop devices.

DOM Size Benchmarks

A larger DOM, with more elements and nodes, will require more parsing time. That will worsen DCL times and measurements later in the loading process. Google's Lighthouse tool warns about DOM size when it exceeds 800 nodes and reports an error when the DOM exceeds 1,400 nodes.[2]

Browser Timings: GTmetrix

The first question to answer is what the DCL time is for a particular page on the website. This can be done using a tool like GTmetrix (`https://gtmetrix.com/`). After running a test, click the "Performance" tab and scroll to the "Browser Timings" section. In the example shown in Figure 3-2, the DCL time was 2.2 seconds. GTmetrix also shows other important metrics and these can help put DCL time in context. In the example shown in Figure 3-2, TTFB was 1.5 seconds. That means 1.5

---

[1] "Report: Loading Speed." HTTP Archive. October 1, 2023. `https://httparchive.org/reports/loading-speed#dcl`

[2] "Avoid an Excessive DOM Size." 2019. Chrome for Developers. Google for Developers. May 2, 2019, updated October 4, 2019. `https://developer.chrome.com/en/docs/lighthouse/performance/dom-size/#how-the-lighthouse-dom-size-audit-fails`

seconds of the 2.2 second DCL time was spent loading the first byte of data. It took the browser 700 milliseconds from when it received the first byte of data (TTFB) to finish parsing the HTML page (DCL time). In this example, then, the best way to reduce DCL time would be to reduce TTFB.

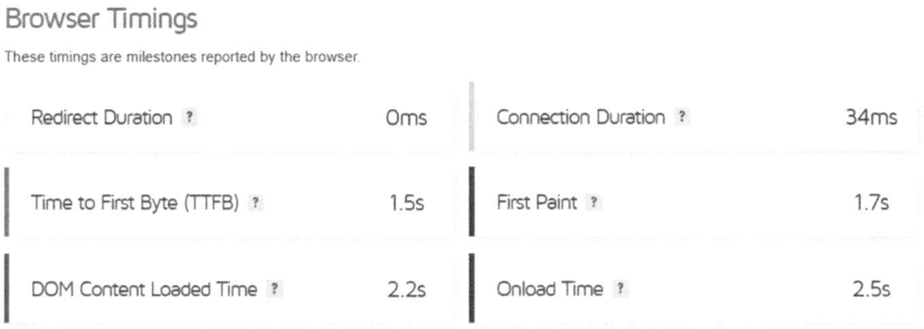

Browser Timings

These timings are milestones reported by the browser.

Redirect Duration ?	0ms	Connection Duration ?	34ms
Time to First Byte (TTFB) ?	1.5s	First Paint ?	1.7s
DOM Content Loaded Time ?	2.2s	Onload Time ?	2.5s

Figure 3-2. *GTmetrix Browser Timings*

GTmetrix also provides options to test on different connection speeds and using different device types. These options can be set by selecting "Analysis Options" before running a test. This is a helpful way to see how, or if, DCL time changes for different types of visitors.

DOM Elements: PageSpeed Insights

A larger DOM size will take longer for the browser to parse, so it is important to measure the total DOM size. Along with providing speed metric data, discussed in Appendix B, PageSpeed Insights (`https://pagespeed.web.dev/`) also provides an evaluation of the website's DOM size as part of the diagnostic information.

After running a test, choose "Mobile" or "Desktop" at the top of the screen to view the DOM size by device. Once a device type is selected, scroll below the performance data to the "Diagnostics" section. If the DOM size exceeds thresholds, a warning or error will be provided about excessive DOM size. The example page shown in Figure 3-3 has a DOM with 4,317 DOM elements. If the DOM size is not listed as a warning or error, that means it is below the thresholds and the DOM size will be listed in the "Passed Audits" section of the report instead.

Figure 3-3. *Diagnostics from PageSpeed Insights*

DOM Nodes: Google Chrome DevTools

Google Chrome's DevTools also shows the DOM size and can be an easier tool to use when testing how to improve DOM size. To access Chrome DevTools, open Google Chrome. Before opening a webpage, right click and choose "Inspect". Once DevTools opens, use the kebab (three vertical dots) menu at the top to choose "More Tools" and open "Performance Monitor" (see Figure 3-4).

Figure 3-4. *How to access Performance Monitor in Chrome DevTools*

This will open the "Performance Monitor" report, as shown in Figure 3-5. In this example, there are 25,958 DOM nodes. Unlike PageSpeed Insights, Chrome DevTools shows total DOM nodes which includes HTML tags along with comments, whitespace, and text.

Figure 3-5. *Chrome Dev Tools Performance Monitor*

The "Performance Monitor" report shows how the DOM size changes when interacting with the page. With the report open, begin scrolling through the page, expanding or collapsing hidden elements, and interacting with any other features to see how the total DOM nodes change. Some interactions will not change the DOM node count and others may change it greatly. This helps identify which parts of the page have a greater impact on DOM size and may be important areas to address to improve DCL time.

For highly dynamic pages, the total DOM nodes may change even when not interacting with the page due to background processes. The timeline to the right of the "Performance Monitor" report shows how DOM nodes change over time, even when not interacting with the page.

Because this is in the browser, as opposed to an external tool like PageSpeed Insights or GTmetrix, this can be used on staging environments or password-restricted pages. This provides an easy way to test the DOM size on new pages. It also makes it easy to test how altering the code by adding or removing features from existing pages can impact DOM size.

Ways to Improve DOMContentLoaded

DCL time includes everything TTFB measures plus the time needed to parse HTML code. If DCL time is high, the first step is to check TTFB. If DCL time is high because of a higher TTFB, then improving TTFB by optimizing the connection to the server and how the server processes code presents a bigger opportunity to improve speed. If TTFB is already within acceptable levels but DCL time is higher, then improving DCL times by reducing DOM size and changing how JavaScript files are loaded presents a bigger opportunity.

HTML Reduction

The best way to speed up HTML parsing is to reduce the amount of HTML code that needs to be parsed. This is often technically challenging. It requires developers to rework how the HTML on each page has been constructed. For HTML directly within the developer's control, there are often ways to recode the HTML to use fewer tags, at least to a certain extent. Options for optimizing the HTML code may be limited if a page has been generated by numerous third-party plugins or page builders. Those plugins and page builders typically do not give developers sufficient access or control to adjust how the HTML is generated.

Reducing HTML code can only go so far to decrease the DOM size. Even if a developer can rework all of the website's HTML code or the best plugins and page builders are used on the website, there is only so much HTML that can be reduced if the webpage contains many content blocks and interactive features. Every content block and interactive feature adds more DOM elements. At a certain point, those content blocks and features need to be reevaluated to determine if their value justifies the impact on DOM size and website speed.

As an example, consider a WordPress website that has an extensive sidebar navigation with links to the latest articles, related tags and categories, a search form, a calendar widget to view articles by date, and more. This sidebar navigation might be generated by a combination of WordPress plugins and the overall settings for the sidebar are controlled by the website's theme. Because of the sidebar's complexity, all those elements in the sidebar add hundreds of elements to the DOM, increasing DCL time. A developer might be able to choose different plugins that reduce DOM size and may be able to adjust the theme files to use slightly less code for the sidebar. However, the only viable option to improve DCL time and reduce DOM size in this example would be evaluating how necessary the sidebar is to determine if the slower speeds are worthwhile given the user experience benefits.

Evaluating the trade-off between speed and user experience starts by determining if visitors are using the sidebar. In this blog sidebar example, that would include questions like: Are visitors clicking on the latest articles? Are visitors using the tag or category pages linked to in the sidebar? Do visitors use the search form? Even if the links and the search form in the sidebar are used, does usage correlate with higher engagement or conversion rates? If those features are not used or do not correlate with higher engagement or conversion rates, then simplifying the sidebar or removing the sidebar altogether could help reduce the DOM size and improve DCL time without harming overall business objectives.

Changing How JavaScript Loads: *Async* and *Defer*

Any JavaScript in an HTML document will, by default, interrupt the HTML parsing process. To improve DCL time, this default behavior can be adjusted by either deferring the JavaScript files or loading JavaScript files asynchronously.

Asynchronous Loading

The asynchronous loading instruction is communicated to the browser with the *async* attribute in the <script> tag.

```
<script async src="functions.js"></script>
```

Loading a JavaScript file asynchronously tells the browser that it does not need to interrupt the HTML parser to request, download, process, and execute that JavaScript file. Instead, the browser will start downloading the JavaScript file while the rest of the HTML parsing continues. When the JavaScript file has been downloaded, the browser will pause the HTML parsing to execute the file. That means asynchronously loaded JavaScript files can still impact DCL if the JavaScript file finishes downloading while the HTML is still being parsed. Figure 3-6 shows an image from Web.dev demonstrating how fetching the asynchronously loaded JavaScript file does not affect parsing but executing that file does. The way asynchronous JavaScript files are loaded also means the file will be ready when it is ready and not necessarily ready in the order presented in the HTML document.

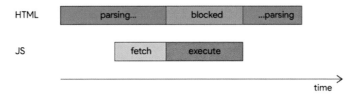

Figure 3-6. *How async impacts the parsing process. Image from* `https://web.dev/articles/efficiently-load-third-party-javascript`

Deferring JavaScript Load

The defer instruction is communicated to the browser with the *defer* attribute in the <script> tag.

```
<script defer src="functions.js"></script>
```

JavaScript files can also be referenced at the end of the HTML document. This effectively defers the load of that file as well because it will be one of the last elements the HTML parser encounters.

Deferring the load of a JavaScript file also tells the browser that it does not need to interrupt the HTML parser to request, download, process, and execute that JavaScript file. Like an asynchronously loaded JavaScript file, the browser will download the deferred JavaScript file while the rest of the HTML parsing continues. The difference between asynchronously loaded and deferred JavaScript files is that the deferred JavaScript file will not be executed until the parsing is completed, instead of interrupting the parsing process. The change to the parsing process when a JavaScript file is deferred is shown in Figure 3-7. As with asynchronously loaded JavaScript files, fetching the deferred file does not interrupt parsing but that file will not be executed until parsing is completed.

Figure 3-7. *How defer impacts the parsing process. Image from*
https://web.dev/articles/efficiently-load-third-party-
javascript

There is an important nuance to consider about deferring as it relates to DCL. The DCL event will only fire in the browser once all deferred JavaScript files have been executed. This means adding defer to JavaScript files can improve how efficiently the HTML code is parsed and may improve DCL time as a result. However, it is also possible that deferring JavaScript files will not necessarily change the DCL time. Instead, the impact of deferring JavaScript files will more consistently be reflected in other metrics, especially First Contentful Paint.

Recap: When to Use DOMContentLoaded

DCL time is useful for diagnosing performance issues to determine how HTML parsing time affects overall website speed.

- **Is the reporting scope meaningful?** DCL time is a bridge between the initial connection to the website and the beginning of the browser presenting website content to the visitor. On its own, DCL time shows the amount of time from the browser making the initial connection until the HTML code is parsed. DCL time needs to be compared against other metrics to be more meaningful. When compared to TTFB, it is clear how much of the initial connection is spent generating the first byte of data and how much time is spent parsing HTML code. Comparing DCL time to First Contentful Paint shows how much delay there is between parsing the HTML code and when visitors can see content painted to the screen (First Contentful Paint will be discussed in Chapter 5). As a result, DCL time is often better to measure during a deeper diagnostic of website speed when it can be compared to these other metrics.

- **Is it an effective business goal?** DCL time is typically not a useful speed KPI because it only indirectly affects business goals, like other early-stage metrics. Also, HTML parsing time is not the biggest problem on most websites. Given this, DCL time should only be reviewed as part of a deeper diagnostic project when other metrics, like Time to First Byte or First Contentful Paint, indicate slower speeds. During that diagnostic project, it is helpful to review DCL time to understand how long it takes the browser to parse the website's HTML code and if that is slowing the website load.

- **Does it describe the user experience?** DCL time begins to describe an aspect of the user experience. When the DCL event is triggered, the browser has everything it needs to begin displaying content to visitors and after this, visitors will start to see the page. A delayed DCL time would delay the presentation to the visitor, negatively impacting the user experience. However, DCL time does not represent anything visitors are able to do on the website and does not represent how quickly visitors can see the website.

- **How easy is it to improve?** A developer may not have complete control of the website's HTML code because of third-party tools, like plugins or page builders. Some necessary features on a webpage may add an excessive number of elements to the DOM but no effective alternatives exist. Given those restrictions, DCL time may need to remain high and loading times will need to be improved elsewhere.

- **How impactful are improvements?** Improving DCL time will speed up the next steps of loading the website, resulting in visitors seeing the website more quickly. An even bigger impact comes from reducing the DOM size. Along with improving DCL time, a smaller DOM size will make it easier and faster for JavaScript to manipulate the DOM to add, remove, or change a given element after a visitor taps, scrolls, swipes, clicks, or interacts in some other way. The impact of DOM size will be discussed more in later chapters, including Chapter 5 about First Contentful Paint and Chapter 10 about Interaction to Next Paint.

CHAPTER 4

Total Requests and Transfer Size

There is more to a webpage than HTML code. As the browser loads and parses the HTML code, it will find references to other file types, including JavaScript, CSS, font, or image files. The browser requests each referenced file from the server. The server processes the request and sends the requested file to the browser. The browser receives the file and then must process it to continue loading the page. Many of these files need to be requested and loaded before any part of the page can be shown to a visitor.

What Total Requests and Transfer Size Measure

Total Requests measures the total number of files, or resources, that the browser requests when loading a webpage.

The total byte size of requested files can be measured using Transfer Size or Resource Size.

- **Transfer Size** measures the total bytes transferred from the server to the browser for the requested files. Files sent by a server might be compressed to reduce the Transfer Size.

© Matthew Edgar 2024
M. Edgar, *Speed Metrics Guide*, https://doi.org/10.1007/979-8-8688-0155-6_4

- **Resource Size** measures the total bytes of the requested file (or resource) once the browser receives the file from the server and decompresses it.

Requested File Types

The files need to be requested and loaded so that the browser can build the webpage. Each file type affects a different aspect of the loading process. The browser needs to parse the HTML code, execute all JavaScript files, parse the CSS code to compute each element's style, calculate how to layout each element, and, finally, paint each element.

- JavaScript files are loaded synchronously by default and will block parsing. If JavaScript files are deferred the file will be executed after the HTML is parsed. JavaScript files can also be loaded asynchronously, meaning the file will load in the background and not block parsing.

- CSS files (external stylesheets) are loaded synchronously by default, though there are ways to load CSS asynchronously. When loaded synchronously, CSS blocks style computation, layout calculation, and painting because the browser needs to download and parse the CSS code to know how to style the webpage.

- Fonts block painting. Fonts are loaded synchronously by default, which means text is hidden by the browser until the font is ready. This results in a Flash of Invisible Text (FOIT). Fonts can also be loaded asynchronously, with the browser using a system font before switching to the website's specified font, which results in a Flash of Unstyled Text (FOUT).

- Images are loaded synchronously by default and can delay painting. When a browser detects the <img> tag's *src* attribute, it will immediately trigger a request for the file. Images can be lazy loaded, meaning the browser will not load the image until the image scrolls into the visible area of the webpage on the visitor's screen. Lazy loaded will be discussed in the next chapter.

- Videos are typically embedded in an iframe. An iframe specifies a separate source URL the browser needs to load, parse, and paint. For example, a video hosted on YouTube could be referenced in the <iframe> tag's *src* attribute. To present the video for visitors, the browser will fetch this file from `www.youtube.com`, parse the associated code, and then paint the video and other associated content. Loading files in an iframe, like a video, can delay painting. Iframes can be lazy loaded to avoid this delay.

Fetch Priority

The browser does not load all files in the order found in the HTML code. Instead, the browser gives certain files a higher load priority than other file types. This is called the browser's fetch priority. The default fetch priority for Google Chrome is shown in Table 4-1.

Table 4-1. *Chrome resource prioritization*

Priority	Files
Highest	The main document (the HTML page)CSS files requested before preloaded imagesFonts
High	Preload font filesJavaScript requested before preloaded imagesImages shown in first viewport
Medium	CSS files requested after preloaded imagesJavaScript files requested after preloaded images
Low	JavaScript files set to async or deferAll other imagesVideosSVG
Lowest	Prefetch

The default fetch priority can be changed using the *fetchpriority* attribute for images, CSS files, or JavaScript files. The *fetchpriority* attribute can be set to high or low to provide the browser with a hint that a specific resource should be moved up or down the priority order. For example, there may be a particular image that should be given a high priority because of how important it is to the page's content. The following code example provides a hint to the browser to load the image with a high priority.

```
<img src="main-page-image.png" fetchpriority="high">
```

In addition, *preload* and *prefetch* can be applied to change the priority. Both *preload* and *prefetch* are added in <link> tags in the page's <head> section.

Elements with *preload* are given a high priority. This is a mandatory directive, not a hint like *fetchpriority*, and should only be used for critical items that are essential when loading the page. For example, this code would preload the main-stylesheet.css file.

```
<link rel="preload" href="main-stylesheet.css" as="style">
```

Elements with *prefetch* are given the lowest priority. A *prefetch* should only be used for non-critical elements that are needed after the visitor begins interacting with the page, like an image or video presented lower on the page.

```
<link rel="prefetch" href="secondary-image.jpg">
```

Compression

Files sent by the server can be compressed. Compression is the process of reducing a file to a smaller size by removing redundant or unnecessary information. This process reduces Transfer Size. When a browser receives a compressed file from a server, it decompresses the file by reversing the compression process to restore the information about that file. As a result, the Resource Size will not be affected by compression.

Compression can be lossy or lossless. Lossy compression reduces the file size by permanently removing some of the resource's information. That information will not be restored during decompression. Lossless compression reduces the size of the file without losing any information, so it can be fully restored during decompression.

How Images Are Compressed

Images often consume a large percentage of the Transfer Size and Resource Size. It is important to choose the correct image format that will present the image at an acceptable quality while also loading the image at a reasonable file size. A large part of the difference in those image formats is in how the image itself is compressed.

A JPEG image uses lossy compression, meaning that some data will be lost from the JPEG image. That is typically acceptable for photographs where some data loss will be visually undetectable. This helps reduce the byte size of JPEG images.

A PNG image uses lossless compression, so no data will be lost from the image. This is important for images with text or sharp lines where any data loss would be visually noticeable. However, that means the transfer and Resource Size of PNG images will be much larger compared to the same image saved as a JPEG.

GIF also uses a lossless compression, but its compression algorithm is less efficient than a PNG file, resulting in larger file sizes. GIF is typically used for animation, but often a compressed GIF file will be larger than an optimized video file showing the same animation.

WebP is a newer format that can use lossless and lossy compression. WebP's lossy and lossless compression are designed to be more efficient than JPEG or PNG. This results in much smaller file sizes for images of a similar quality. WebP images can be animated making this an alternative to GIF files.

AVIF is the newest format. Browser support is growing, but Google does not currently support this format when crawling or indexing images on websites. Like WebP, AVIF can use lossless or lossy compression. However, AVIF has been designed to compress files better than WebP, resulting in smaller files of a similar image quality level.

How Other Files Are Compressed

Other requested files can be compressed as well. The two most common compression methods on the web today are Gzip and Brotli with 88.7% of websites using some form of compression – 58.8% of websites use Gzip compression and 43.3% use Brotli compression.[1]

The first version of Gzip compression was released in 1993 and is an all-purpose compression algorithm that will reduce the overall byte size of any file type, including HTML, JS, or CSS files. Gzip is lossless, so no data will be lost due to the compression.

---

[1] "Usage Statistics of Compression for Websites." 2023. W3Techs. Q-Success. November 20, 2023. https://w3techs.com/technologies/details/ce-compression

Brotli was developed by Google in 2013 and it was designed specifically to work with website files. It uses similar underlying DEFLATE algorithms like Gzip, but Brotli uses additional techniques, like data dictionaries, to more efficiently compress files. Like Gzip, Brotli is lossless.

Most studies have found that Brotli compresses files more effectively than Gzip. However, the difference between the two is often negligible for most websites. The more important step is having some form of compression enabled.

Measuring Total Requests and Transfer Size

Some pages have only limited functionality and no images, so there will be few files that need to be requested to load these types of pages. Other pages may have dozens of images and lots of complex functionality, requiring more requested files. Total Requests and Transfer Size should be measured across multiple pages to account for these differences. Requested files can also change depending on the device type. For example, images might be removed from the mobile version of a webpage or JavaScript loads differently depending on the device type. To understand how the website load changes per device type, both Total Requests and Transfer Size should be measured on desktop and mobile devices.

Total Request Benchmarks

According to data from HTTP Archive looking at millions of websites, the median mobile website requests 67 files and the median desktop website requests 71 files.[2] From the same data, 10% of evaluated websites load no more than 21 files on mobile websites and 22 files on desktop websites,

---

[2] "Report: Page Weight." HTTP Archive. October 1, 2023. `https://httparchive.org/reports/page-weight`

though 75% of websites load as many as 107 files on mobile websites and 113 files on desktop websites. Table 4-2 shows Total Requests by requested file type for 75th percentile of websites.

Table 4-2. *Total Requests by file type – data from HTTP Archive, Page Weight Report*

File Type	Desktop (75th percentile)	Mobile (75th percentile)
CSS	15	15
Fonts	7	6
Images	37	34
JavaScript	40	38

Transfer Size Benchmarks

The median Transfer Size for all requested files for mobile websites is 2.2 megabytes and is 2.4 megabytes for desktop websites, according to HTTP Archive's dataset.[3] Table 4-3 shows the Transfer Size by request type (measured in kilobytes) for the 75th percentile of websites. As with the total number of requests, JavaScript and images contribute the most to Transfer Size.

---

[3] Ibid.

Table 4-3. *Transfer Size by file type – data from HTTP Archive, Page Weight Report – all data shown in kilobytes (KB)*

File Type	Desktop (75th percentile)	Mobile (75th percentile)
CSS	156.1	150.2
Fonts	277.0	244.5
Images	2739.2	2424.0
JavaScript	1096.8	1017.4

Transfer Size and Resource Size: Chrome DevTools

Chrome's DevTools area shows all files requested for a page, along with data about each requested file. Before opening a webpage, right click in the Chrome interface and click Inspect to open Chrome's DevTools. Once this opens, click "Network" in the top bar. "Network" may be hidden from view but can be accessed by clicking the ">>" icon. After it opens, load the webpage to test in Chrome. As the webpage loads, the resources requested for the page to load are listed in the table presented on the "Network" panel.

Once all requests have been made, the bottom of the table shows the total number of requests (labeled "requests"), the Transfer Size (labeled "transferred"), and the Resource Size (labeled "resources"). In Figure 4-1, there were 20 requested files with a total Transfer Size of 430 kilobytes and an uncompressed Resource Size of 1 megabyte. This example also shows the "Priority" column, representing the priority given to each requested resource. This column is not shown by default but can be shown by right-clicking the column headers and choosing "Priority."

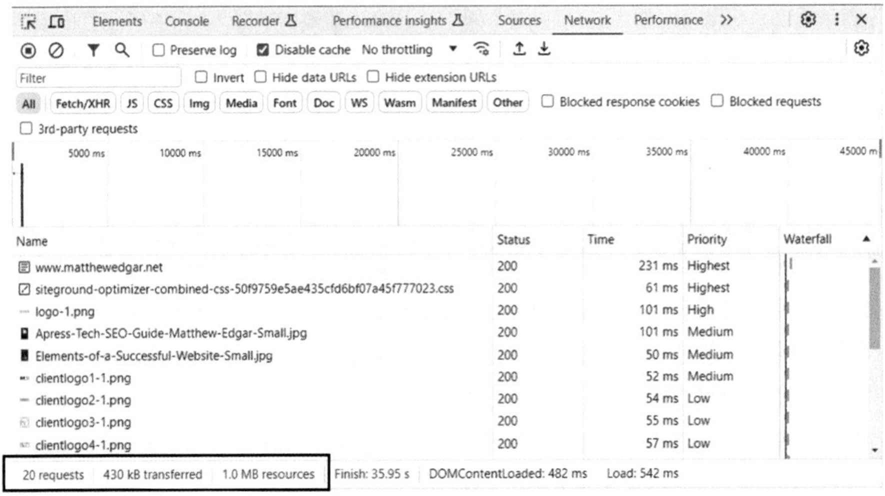

Figure 4-1. *Chrome DevTools Network Report*

The top of the "Network" panel provides functionality to filter to specific file types or a text box to filter to files with a certain name. The filters are helpful to see these metrics for specific types of resources. For example, Figure 4-2 shows this report filtered to JavaScript files (JS). JavaScript files only account for 15% of Total Requests with 3 requested files but account for 50%, or 215 kilobytes, of the total Transfer Size.

Figure 4-2. *Chrome DevTools – Filter Network Report*

Total Requests by Type: WebPageTest

WebPageTest (www.webpagetest.org/) can test Transfer Size and Total Requests for a variety of devices and browsers. After running a speed test in WebPageTest, select "Content" from the "View menu" to access the "Content Breakdown" report. An example is shown in Figure 4-3. This report includes a "Breakdown by MIME type," which shows the requests by file type and the total bytes consumed for each file type. In the "Bytes" table, the "Bytes" column shows the Transfer Size and the "Uncompressed" column shows the Resource Size for each file type. The "Requests" table shows a count of how many total files of each type were loaded.

Breakdown by MIME type

First View:

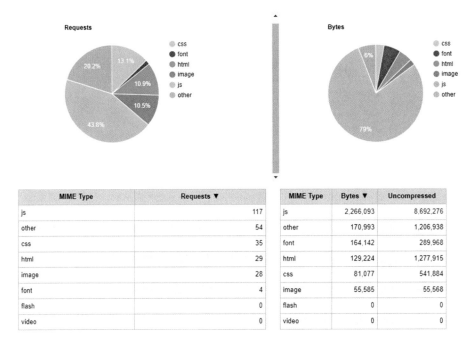

MIME Type	Requests ▼
js	117
other	54
css	35
html	29
image	28
font	4
flash	0
video	0

MIME Type	Bytes ▼	Uncompressed
js	2,266,093	8,692,276
other	170,993	1,206,938
font	164,142	289,968
html	129,224	1,277,915
css	81,077	541,884
image	55,585	55,568
flash	0	0
video	0	0

Figure 4-3. *WebPageTest Content Breakdown Report*

In this example, the "Requests" table shows there are 117 JavaScript files requested and the "Bytes" table shows JavaScript files have a 2.26 megabyte Transfer Size. This is well above the median and 75th percentile amounts seen in HTTP Archive's dataset. There are also 54 Other files with a Transfer Size just over 170 kilobytes. Other file types include configuration files, data files, or files with some other non-standard type.

Ways to Improve Total Requests and Transfer Size

The primary focus is to reduce Transfer Size. Loading many files that have a smaller Transfer Size will have less of an impact on the webpage's speed than loading a few files that have a very large Transfer Size. If five images are saved at smaller file sizes, there will still be five images to load but they will have a smaller Transfer Size allowing those images to load faster. The same is true for JavaScript or CSS files that can be minified or compressed to load at a smaller Transfer Size without changing Total Requests. That said, reducing Total Requests is one way to reduce Transfer Size. Consolidating multiple files or removing unnecessary files will reduce Total Requests while also improving Transfer Size.

Consolidating Multiple JavaScript or CSS Files

One common speed optimization recommendation is to consolidate, or concatenate, multiple files into a single file. Instead of loading five CSS files, the browser loads a single CSS file that contains the code from all five files. This is not always an appropriate optimization tactic. The recommendation stems from the "head of line blocking" problem that existed in HTTP/1. Think of every file the browser needs to request to load a webpage lined up in a queue. In HTTP/1, the browser was only able to request a single file at a time from that queue and each file in the front of the line would block other files from loading. The longer the line, the longer it would take the browser to load the webpage. With this problem in mind, it made sense to keep the line as short as possible by reducing Total Requests.

However, the newer version of HTTP, HTTP/2, changed this consideration by introducing multiplexing. Multiplexing fixes the "head of line blocking" problem by allowing multiple files to be requested from the server by the browser simultaneously. Essentially, multiplexing allows the browser to process requested files in multiple queues to load the website more quickly. As a result, splitting JavaScript code into multiple smaller files can often be loaded faster than a larger consolidated file, even if that increases the total number of requested files.

HTTP/2 also allows the browser to progressively load the webpage. As each file is loaded, the browser can process that code and display a portion of the page before loading the next file. If, instead, the browser had to wait for a larger, consolidated file to fully load before displaying any part of the page, visitors would see a blank screen for a longer time.

In some cases, though, consolidation is sensible to support more efficient loading and displaying of the page. For example, a webpage might rely on three small JavaScript files that all work together to load and display one section of the page. Because the browser would always need to download and execute these three JavaScript files before displaying that section, consolidating those files together could likely help improve how quickly the browser is able to display that section of the page. By consolidating, the browser has all the necessary code to execute at once instead of receiving code from different files that may load at different times.

In short, multiple JavaScript files or multiple CSS files can often load faster in HTTP/2 than a single, consolidated JavaScript file or a single, consolidated CSS file – within reason. Even with multiplexing, a webpage loading hundreds of JavaScript files would make an excessive number of file requests that would slow the website. Consolidation of some requested files is still important to avoid excessive requests. It is useful to test file consolidation, especially to combine smaller script files that are used together.

Domain Sharding and Third-Party Hosts

Another common recommendation is to split resources across multiple domains or subdomains instead of self-hosting all resources on the primary domain. Browsers previously limited connections available per domain; they could only download so many files from that domain at once. A workaround was to load some resources on a different domain, allowing the browser to load files from the primary domain and the other domain concurrently. Resources hosted on a different domain require an extra DNS lookup and an additional TCP connection, but because the browser limited connections per domain, it was faster to make connections to multiple domains when requesting files.

This practice, referred to as domain sharding, is no longer recommended with HTTP/2. With HTTP/2, the browser can make additional, concurrent requests for a single domain, negating the need for sharding. With HTTP/2, the additional DNS lookup and TCP connection times will slow down resource loading without any benefits to performance. Typically, it is better to self-host all files on the primary domain and avoid the additional DNS lookup and TCP connection.

The exception is if the third-party domain is a Content Delivery Network (CDN), which can be used to host font, image, or other static files. The CDN's servers are configured to improve overall load time by offering better server locations, more effective resource caching, decreasing data volume, and more. A browser would need to establish a connection to the CDN's domain or subdomain, but the benefits of the CDN typically offset that additional time required and improve overall performance.

Make the Files Smaller: Minification

It is important to reduce the Transfer Size as much as possible for all requested files. The smaller a file's Transfer Size, the more quickly the browser can download and process that file. Compression is one means of reducing Transfer Size. Another method to reduce Transfer Size is minification. Where compression rewrites the file to send it to the browser in a compressed format, minification is the process of making the original file smaller. As a result, minification reduces Resource Size as well as Transfer Size.

Minification makes the file smaller by removing white space, unnecessary characters, and comments within the code. Minification can also rename longer variable names. For example, here is a simple JavaScript function before and after minification. The minified code performs the same operation but with a 75% smaller Resource Size.

```
// Before minification
function applyDiscount(originalPrice, discountRate) {
  const discountedPrice = originalPrice * (1 - discountRate);
  return discountedPrice;
}

// After minification
function applyDiscount(n,t){return n*(1-t)}
```

Minification can be applied programmatically. For example, several WordPress plugins will minify JavaScript or CSS code. There are also plenty of free tools available that will minify JavaScript or CSS code if a programmatic solution is not feasible, including minify-js.com and minify-css.com.

When to Use Total Requests and Transfer Size

Total Requests and Transfer Size are important to regularly monitor across key pages of the website to detect any major changes.

- **Is the reporting scope meaningful?** Total Requests and Transfer Size define the page's size. A larger page size delays how quickly the page can be displayed to visitors. Monitoring Total Requests and total Transfer Size is a helpful way to see how the webpage changes over time. A sudden increase in Total Requests or Transfer Size needs to be investigated to understand how, and if, those increases affect the website's speed. During that investigation, these metrics can be broken out by file type to see which types of files impact page speed the most. Total Requests and Transfer Size should also be evaluated during website redevelopments or redesigns to see how the new website has changed the loading process.

- **Is it an effective business goal?** What Total Requests and Transfer Size lack is a clear objective. With other metrics discussed in the book, the goal is to make the number smaller. However, given multiplexing in HTTP/2, sometimes more files will load faster than fewer files. Similarly, Transfer Size can only be reduced so far before removing site functionality that negatively affects traffic or conversions. A modern, fully featured shopping cart will require extensive JavaScript and CSS code. The extensive code will increase Transfer Size, but simplifying the functionality or design of the shopping cart to reduce Transfer Size may worsen the user experience to such an extent that it will deter customers from placing orders. Sometimes more extensive code and a larger Transfer Size is better for the business. These technical nuances make it challenging to connect Transfer Size and Total

Requests to business goals. As a result, these metrics are best used by technical teams to monitor website performance, but not as a key metric to share with a wider group of stakeholders.

- **Does it describe the user experience?** Total Requests and Transfer Size do not directly describe the experience visitors have on the website. However, higher Total Requests or larger Transfer Size are often the underlying reason visitors experience slower load times. JavaScript files slow HTML parsing. CSS files slow layout calculations. Fonts and images slow painting. As a result, Total Requests and Transfer Size are an important area to measure to identify which file types, or which specific files, have the biggest impact on website load times. As well, the user experience is heavily influenced by the fetch priority. It is important to ensure that the most critical files visitors need to see are given an appropriate priority.

- **How easy is it to improve?** It is relatively straightforward (if not always technically simple) to remove or consolidate files, add compression, minify JavaScript or CSS code, change fetch priority, and more – especially for self-hosted files. However, these solutions are often blocked by bigger strategic questions behind each change. As an example, additional tracking code can help the business better understand customer behavior, but that tracking code relies on JavaScript and is hosted on a third-party domain. This increases Transfer Size and Total Requests, along with adding another DNS lookup and TCP connection. There is only so much that can be done technically to improve how that tracking code loads. The business needs to decide if the benefits the tracking code provides are worth the speed implications. These types of critical, strategic questions need to be answered for each requested file. It takes time to appropriately test and evaluate the necessity of each requested file, which complicates optimization work.

- **How impactful are improvements?** The biggest impact comes from reducing Transfer Size. Reducing Transfer Size of synchronously loaded JavaScript files, CSS, images, and font files will improve other speed metrics, especially metrics reporting on how quickly the browser painted the website. Reducing Transfer Size also means visitors will be able to see and interact with the page more quickly and that can result in improvements to conversion and engagement rates.

CHAPTER 5

First Contentful Paint

As the browser requests and receives the files needed for the webpage, it processes these files to extract the information it needs to begin building the webpage. The process of the browser building the webpage is known as rendering. During rendering, the browser converts all the files it has received and all the code it has processed into a functioning webpage. The last step of the rendering process is painting, or displaying, the webpage element by element. When the browser starts painting elements, visitors finally begin to see something on the website and are no longer looking at a blank screen.

What First Contentful Paint Measures

First Contentful Paint (FCP) measures the time between the initial request for the website and the time the browser paints the first pixels of content on the screen.

© Matthew Edgar 2024
M. Edgar, *Speed Metrics Guide*, https://doi.org/10.1007/979-8-8688-0155-6_5

Critical Rendering Path

The critical rendering path is the initial sequence browsers take to convert the code received from the server into a page displayed on the visitor's screen. The rendering process is shown in Figure 5-1 and includes the following:

- **Parse:** The browser receives and parses the HTML code from the server. During parsing, the browser loads JavaScript files and executes JavaScript code. Using the HTML received from the server and any changes made to that HTML by the JavaScript code, the browser constructs the Document Object Model (DOM).

- **Style:** The browser also loads CSS files referenced in the HTML file from the server. After loading the CSS files, the browser parses the CSS code to construct the CSS Object Model (CSSOM). The CSSOM contains the style instructions for every element in the DOM, such as the element's font size or color.

- **Layout:** After the CSSOM is constructed, the browser brings the DOM and CSSOM together in the render tree. The render tree contains information about all visible elements on the page. The browser uses the render tree to calculate the position and size of each element on the page. With this information, the browser determines how to create the visual layout of the webpage.

- **Paint:** The browser finishes loading fonts and image files, then the browser paints, or displays, all visual elements to the webpage. The first content painted will trigger FCP.

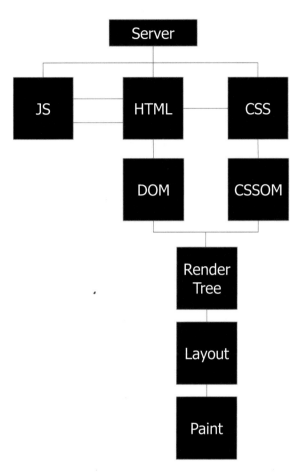

Figure 5-1. *Critical Rendering Path*

FCP represents the beginning of the final step in the critical rendering path, indicating when visitors begin to see something appear on the page. FCP also marks the transition into the middle stages of loading the webpage – when painting starts, visitors begin to see the page.

How the browser parses HTML to construct the DOM was discussed in Chapter 3, and how the browser loads the files needed to construct the page was discussed in Chapter 4. The remainder of the critical rendering path is discussed in this chapter.

CSS Object Model (CSSOM) and Style Calculation

After parsing the HTML, the browser next determines how to style the elements contained in the HTML. To do this, the browser needs to parse the CSS code. After parsing the CSS, the browser constructs the CSSOM and uses that to compute the style for all DOM elements.

As discussed in Chapter 3, the DOM will change as JavaScript is loaded and executed. Because of this, the DOM is built in an incremental process. In contrast, CSSOM construction is not an incremental process. CSS rules may redeclare or refine styles for certain elements, so the browser must load and parse all the CSS code to know what the styles are and to build the CSSOM. As a result, the browser will block the next steps of loading the page until the CSSOM is fully constructed, resulting in a slower FCP.

The more complex the CSS or the larger the CSS files, the longer this process will take. It will also take longer for the browser to parse CSS code that contains conflicting rules. In addition, some styles can add to the complexity as well. For example, if the CSS relies heavily on gradients or shadows, that will require more time for the browser to calculate and apply those styles. Simplifying the CSS code and reducing the number of CSS files used can help speed up this process.

Layout and Reflow

After constructing the DOM and CSSOM, the browser combines the two into a render tree. The browser uses the render tree to calculate the page's layout. To begin calculating layout, the browser determines the dimensions, or width and height, of the visitor's device. With the device dimensions, the browser then moves through the DOM to identify the size and position of each visible element. This includes information about where that element is placed on the page, how much space each element needs, and how each element relates to each other. Because the layout process moves through the DOM, a larger DOM size can slow this process and slow FCP.

After completing the initial layout calculations, the browser may need to recalculate the page's layout if any changes are made to the DOM. As an example, a page's HTML code may not specify the width or height of an image, so the browser does not know the size of the image when it initially calculates the layout of the page. Without the image dimensions, the browser specifies a default space for the image. Once the image is loaded, the browser can determine the image dimensions and uses that information to recalculate the layout to adjust the positions of all other elements on the webpage accordingly.

This recalculation process is known as reflow. Reflows require the browser to do an extensive amount of work recalculating how elements are sized and where elements are positioned on the page. This additional work calculating the page layout can keep the browser busy and delay painting, resulting in a slower FCP. Limiting excessive reflows can help improve the browser's performance when loading the page and that helps improve FCP.

Content Evaluated by FCP

Once the layout process is completed, the browser begins painting text, images, videos, borders, colors, and all other visual elements. FCP is triggered only when specific types of content are painted: text, images, background images, non-white SVG elements, or non-white canvas elements.

Figure 5-2 shows when FCP occurs. Visitors previously saw a blank screen, but FCP marks the appearance of the header background and website logo. As this example demonstrates, the content that appears at FCP may not be meaningful for visitors. In this example, visitors would know that the website is loading but would not have any meaningful elements to interact with or important text to read at FCP.

Figure 5-2. *FCP time as shown in WebPageTest's filmstrip report*

Related Metrics: Start Render and First Paint

Start Render measures when any visible element appears on the page. In contrast, FCP measures when only specific types of elements appear on the page. Start Render can only be measured in synthetic or simulated testing environments. These testing tools analyze a video of the website loading to detect when the first element is painted. FCP can be measured in simulated environments but, unlike Start Render, can also be measured for real-world visitors to the website. A way of measuring FCP for real-world visitors is discussed in Appendix B.

First Paint also measures when the browser paints the page's first element but uses a broader definition for content than FCP. First Paint is triggered when anything different than the default background color is painted. This is similar to Start Render, but unlike Start Render, First Paint can be measured for real visitors and in a simulated environment.

Because Start Render and First Paint detect when anything is painted, they may not always be useful metrics to understand the visitor's experience watching the page load. While that means these are often not metrics to regularly monitor, Start Render or First Paint are useful metrics to review in a deeper diagnostic of page speed to identify delays in the painting process. For example, Start Render or First Paint may occur several hundred milliseconds before FCP. Normally, these three metrics occur at almost the same time. When FCP happens much later, this means the painting process started with something being painted, triggering Start Render and First Paint, but there was a delay painting the specific types of content FCP evaluates. Determining what is causing that delay would surface ways of improving FCP.

How Fonts Affect Painting

There are two types of fonts that can be used in a website's design: system fonts and custom fonts.

System fonts, or web safe fonts, are fonts that are already loaded on a visitor's device. This includes fonts like Arial or Times New Roman. Because the font is already available on the visitor's devices, the server does not need to send any files associated with that font to the browser. The browser can begin painting the text styled with system fonts more quickly.

However, most websites do not use system fonts, instead using custom fonts that match the company's branding to create a better website design. Unlike system fonts, the browser will need to download the files associated with every custom font used by this webpage. As mentioned in Chapter 4, by default, browsers will wait until all custom font files have loaded before painting any text using those custom fonts. This can result in a Flash of Invisible Text (FOIT) where the text remains hidden until the browser is able to load the font files and apply the appropriate font style.

Measuring First Contentful Paint

Each page will contain different images, script files, and distinct elements with unique styling. Those differences change how each page is rendered and change what elements are painted first. FCP should be measured on different pages of the website or, if templates are used, FCP can be tested on a sample of pages using each template. FCP should also be evaluated across mobile and desktop devices, including devices with slower processing times, because these differences will impact how quickly the browser moves through the critical rendering path.

FCP Benchmarks

Google Developer guidelines recommend webpages have an FCP under 1.8 seconds to be considered fast and an FCP over 3 seconds will be considered slow.[1] According to HTTP Archive, the median mobile website has an FCP of 3.8 seconds and the median desktop website has an FCP of 2.3 seconds.[2]

Visualizing FCP: GTmetrix and WebPageTest

The best way to understand FCP is with a visual report. GTmetrix and WebPageTest both offer a visual timeline showing when FCP occurs and what content is painted first.

After running a report in GTmetrix (`https://gtmetrix.com/`), the "Summary" tab includes a "Speed Visualization" report. FCP is indicated

---

[1] "First Contentful Paint." 2019. Chrome for Developers. Google for Developers. May 2, 2019, updated June 4, 2021. `https://developer.chrome.com/en/docs/lighthouse/performance/first-contentful-paint/#how-lighthouse-determines-your-fcp-score`

[2] "Report: Loading Speed." HTTP Archive. October 1, 2023. `https://httparchive.org/reports/loading-speed#fcp`

on the relevant part of the timeline and the visualization will show what content was painted first. The visualization also includes other timings, such as Time to First Byte (TTFB). An example visualization is shown in Figure 5-3 with FCP occurring at 1.3 seconds. Under the "Performance" tab, GTmetrix provides the specific timings, including First Paint.

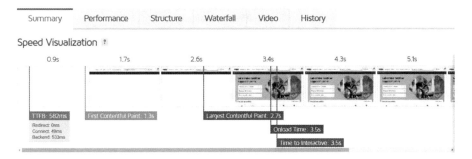

Figure 5-3. *GTmetrix – Speed Visualization*

WebPageTest (`www.webpagetest.org/`) also reports on FCP and shows a timeline. Unlike GTmetrix, WebPageTest shows the Start Render time. After running a test, FCP is included as one of the Page Performance Metrics. WebPageTest also presents a timeline of the Visual Page Loading Process at .10 second intervals, showing what content was painted first. In Figure 5-4, this website has an FCP of 3.637 seconds and a Start Render of 3.6 seconds. The "Visual Page Load Process" highlights the painting starting at the 3.6-second mark and shows what was painted first.

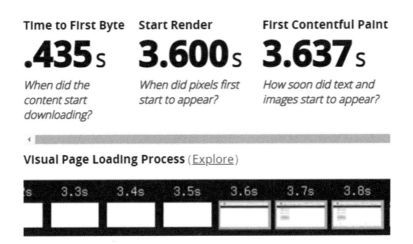

Figure 5-4. *WebPageTest – Page Performance Metrics and Visual Page Loading Process*

Critical Rendering Path Details: Chrome DevTools

There are many steps in the critical rendering path. It is important to understand which of those steps consumes the most time. The time consumed for these steps can be viewed using Chrome DevTools.

To access Chrome DevTools, open Google Chrome. Before opening a webpage, right click and choose "Inspect". In the top menu bar, choose "Performance" (this may require clicking the ">>" icon first). On the "Performance" tab, click the record button and then go to the address bar to load the webpage. Chrome will now record the webpage loading process.

Once Chrome finishes loading the page, DevTools will process the recording and load the report in the DevTools "Performance" panel. Look for the "Summary" section that is shown in Figure 5-5. This summary shows the amount of time the browser spent at various stages of the critical rendering path:

- **Loading:** load files and parse the HTML code

- **Scripting:** execute all JavaScript files

- **Rendering:** compute styles and calculate layout

- **Painting:** painting the page – this is all painting, not exclusively FCP

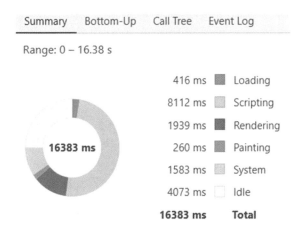

Figure 5-5. *Chrome DevTools performance summary*

In the example shown, the bulk of time was spent with Scripting, when the browser was processing this webpage's JavaScript files. This suggests this website's FCP can be improved by optimizing JavaScript. Rendering times are also higher, so optimizing CSS may also be an opportunity. More research would need to be done into which specific CSS files or JavaScript functions are contributing the most to this time, but this report can help narrow the scope of optimization projects.

Ways to Improve First Contentful Paint

FCP is a middle-stage metric, with many load operations happening prior to FCP. As a result, there are many ways to approach improving a slower FCP. Optimizing the server's performance to reduce TTFB will improve FCP as well. Optimizing HTML code to improve DOMContentLoaded Time or to reduce the size of the DOM will speed up parsing and allow the browser to paint the page more quickly. Reducing Transfer Size and Total Requests will reduce how much work the browser needs to do when loading the page, resulting in faster paint times. Optimizing CSS or JavaScript code to speed up style and layout calculations can help improve painting too. Along with these changes, FCP can also be improved by loading fonts and images more efficiently.

Font Loading: Avoiding FOIT and FOUT

If custom fonts are used, the goal is to avoid a Flash of Invisible Text (FOIT) while the browser waits for the custom font file to load. FOIT means visitors are unable to see any text on the page, delaying when visitors can begin using the page. The best way to avoid FOIT is to select a fallback font. The browser can use the fallback font until the custom font has been loaded and is ready for use. The fallback font allows the browser to paint the text more quickly. The fallback font should be a system font that does not need to be downloaded to the browser.

The problem is that the fallback font will create a new problem, referred to as the Flash of Unstyled Text (FOUT). With FOUT, visitors see the font in a different style before the custom font loads. While FOIT and FOUT are both a problem, FOIT is typically a worse problem because at least with FOUT, visitors can begin to read the text even though it is not styled appropriately. FOUT can become a bigger problem if the text shifts when the browser updates the text to use the custom font. The custom font might use a different size, kerning, or weight than the fallback font.

To minimize the impact of FOUT, steps can be taken to reduce how much the text changes between the fallback and custom font styles. The fallback system font can be styled to closely match the appearance of the custom font. Tools like the "Font style matcher" (`https://meowni.ca/font-style-matcher/`), shown in Figure 5-6, can be used to style a system font so that it closely matches the custom font. This tool shows an overlap of the two styles – the more the two fonts overlap, the less shifting will occur when the custom font file eventually loads.

Figure 5-6. *Font style matcher – construct a fallback font that closely matches the custom font –* `https://meowni.ca/font-style-matcher/`

The instructions for the fallback font are provided in the CSS code with *font-display* defined in the *@font-face* rules. This code sets the *font-display* is set to *swap*, as in the following code example. This tells the browser to paint the text in the fallback font before swapping to the custom font when the custom font file is loaded.

```
<style>
/* Define the custom font (Custom Font) */
@font-face {
  font-family: 'Custom Font';
```

```
  src: local('Custom Font'), url('path/to/custom-font.woff2')
format('woff2');
  font-display: swap;
}

/* Use Arial as the fallback font */
body {
  font-family: 'Custom Font', Arial, sans-serif;
}
</style>
```

Setting the *font-display* rule to *swap* is not the only option. The *font-display* rule instructs the browser how long to hide (or block) the text and how long to allow for swapping out the font. A *swap* setting instructs the browser to not block the text from appearing and to allow an unlimited amount of time for swapping the font. The *swap* setting avoids FOIT because it specifically tells the browser to display the text as quickly as possible using the fallback font and then tells the browser to swap out the font style whenever the font file happens to load.

Other *font-display* settings can be used. For better performance, *font-display* can be set to *optional*, which gives the browser an extremely short window, typically 100 milliseconds, to download the custom font file and during that window, the text is hidden. This resolves FOUT and FOIT but may result in the custom font never being used if that file is not loaded in the window provided. Alternatively, if style is a greater priority than performance, the *block* setting prevents painting the text for a longer period, giving the browser more time to download the custom font file. This increases FOIT but minimizes FOUT. Table 5-1 summarizes the available *font-display* settings.

Table 5-1. *Summarizing available font-display settings*

Setting	Font Swap Time	Block (or Hide) Text Time
auto	Default to the browser settings	Default to the browser settings
block	Infinite (swaps when font loads)	Short block period (3 seconds)
swap	Infinite (swaps when font loads)	Zero seconds (paint text immediately in fallback font)
fallback	Short (swap only if custom font file loads in a short period, typically 3 seconds)	Extremely small (100ms or less)
optional	Zero second (no swap, custom font only used if painted in small block period)	Extremely small (100ms or less)

Regardless of the *font-display* setting used, it is important to load the custom font file as quickly as possible. Self-hosted custom fonts can typically load faster than fonts hosted by third-party services. If the font file is hosted by a third-party service, the browser will need to look up the DNS information for that third-party service's domain and establish a TCP connection with that domain. This can be done with a *preconnect* tag, as discussed in Chapter 1. The *preconnect* tag should only be used for critical files. Font files are typically critical files to load because of the impact on painting. The following code example uses a *preconnect* tag to establish a connection to Google Fonts. This code would be placed in the <head> of the webpage's HTML.

```
<link rel="preconnect" href="https://fonts.googleapis.com" />
```

Lazy Load: Image and Iframe

Images are often one of the biggest contributors to a webpage's total transfer size. Because of this, images can slow the critical rendering path by blocking other resources and consuming the browser's processing time. This delays painting, slowing FCP.

Images do not necessarily need to be loaded when the page first loads. Any images presented lower on the page will not be seen by visitors unless they scroll and may not be seen at all if visitors do not scroll. Having the browser spend time loading an image the visitor might not see unnecessarily wastes time. Instead of loading images when the page loads, it makes more sense to delay loading the image until, and if, the image is needed. This can be done with lazy loading.

With lazy loading, the browser waits to load the image until the visitor scrolls down the page and is closer to the part of the page where the image is displayed. The browser then makes a request for the image, downloads it, and paints the image. This avoids loading a larger file on the initial load. If a visitor does not scroll, then the image would never be loaded. These savings in the initial load time can result in a faster FCP.

Previously, a JavaScript library needed to handle image lazy loading. Given how JavaScript files contribute to slower speeds, loading a JavaScript file to optimize image loading did not always result in an overall gain. If anything, the JavaScript library could delay parsing, resulting in a slower FCP.

There is now an alternative to using the JavaScript library: the *loading* attribute on an <img> tag. Chrome has supported this attribute for years. Edge has supported it since 2020. In 2023, Safari and Firefox began supporting the image loading attribute as well. This can be added to images as shown in the following example.

```
<img src="my-image.jpg" loading="lazy">
```

The loading attribute can also be added to iframes. An iframe embeds another page into the primary page being loaded. The browser needs to load the URL specified in the <iframe> tag's *src* attribute to understand what adjustments need to be made to the primary page when constructing the DOM. As a result, an iframe can block the critical rendering path. As with images, iframe content is not needed until the visitor scrolls to the iframe. The same loading="lazy" attribute can be added to all iframe tags to delay loading and painting the iframe's contents until the visitor scrolls down the page and the iframe comes into view.

When lazy loading images or iframes, it is important to only apply the *loading="lazy"* attribute to elements that are not presented in the first section of content shown on a visitor's screen. This is referred to as the initial viewport. Images in the initial viewport need to be available immediately for the browser to correctly calculate styles and compute the layout. The *loading="lazy"* attribute would delay the image load, resulting in slower style and layout times. Instead, images and iframes in the initial viewport need to load as quickly as possible.

When to Use First Contentful Paint

FCP should be regularly monitored to track the duration of the critical rendering path and identify if any problems need to be investigated further.

- **Is the reporting scope meaningful?** FCP represents the beginning of the end of the critical rendering path, making it an important metric to regularly monitor. This is when visitors will start to see the page. FCP does have a broader scope, measuring everything from the initial connection to the first content appearing on the screen. Everything in the earlier stages of loading the website – DNS lookup times, TCP connection times, server processing times, HTML parsing time, and more – all contribute to FCP. This can make it less actionable than other metrics. If FCP time is high, it is not immediately obvious why until other metrics are evaluated. FCP could be higher due to excessive reflows

89

or complicated CSS code. Or FCP could be higher because TTFB is higher. Monitoring FCP alongside TTFB can help separate out what is contributing more to slower load times.

- **Is it an effective business goal?** Because FCP represents an important milestone during the website loading process, it can be a useful speed KPI. FCP is better connected to core business goals as well. A common business goal is to increase website conversions and if visitors can view the website more quickly, they will be able to interact with the website and convert quicker. FCP is also a more meaningful metric to share with stakeholders. FCP can be represented visually using the timelines to show the time between the initial connection and something appearing on the page.

- **Does it describe the user experience?** FCP, in many respects, is where the user experience truly begins. Before FCP, the user experience was staring at a blank screen waiting for something to appear. The visualizations in GTmetrix or WebPageTest help make clear just how much time people spent looking at that blank screen. However, FCP does not describe anything meaningful about how visitors engaged with the website.

- **How easy is it to improve?** The critical rendering path requires carefully managing what files are loaded and how they are loaded to the webpage. That means a lot of the critical rendering path can be heavily optimized by developers and designers by choosing to use faster loading fonts, changing how images are loaded, writing simpler JavaScript or CSS code, or even altering how files are loaded. However, some platforms restrict how much developers or designers can optimize the underlying code. Certain code libraries cannot be altered without causing bigger problems or preventing future upgrades. Modifications can be made to how many third-party scripts are loaded, but those changes may impact what those third-party scripts do. In short, there are many options available to improve FCP, but there are also many obstacles to address when optimizing FCP.

- **How impactful are improvements?** A faster FCP means the browser will be able to start painting more quickly. If the browser begins painting faster, that will speed up the later stages of the website load. Also, improving FCP often necessitates improving earlier stage metrics, like DCL time or TTFB. Optimizing FCP will typically improve those other metrics too, resulting in even greater impacts on performance.

PART III

Completing the Website Load

CHAPTER 6

Time to Interactive and Total Blocking Time

After the browser paints the page's first content, the browser still needs to paint the remainder of the content. Before it can paint an additional pixel, though, the browser needs to continue doing the work discussed in the previous chapters. That includes executing additional JavaScript, calculating layout changes, and loading additional resource files. While the browser is doing this work, visitors have begun to see elements appear on the page and, seeing these elements, visitors will want to begin interacting with the page. If the browser is still busy rendering the page, it will be unable to respond quickly to a visitor's interactions. This can lead to significant and frustrating delays for visitors.

What Time to Interactive and Total Blocking Time Measure

Time to Interactive (TTI) measures the time after First Contentful Paint (FCP), when the webpage is capable of quickly and reliably responding to visitor interactions. Interactions include taps, clicks, scrolls, and form inputs.

Total Blocking Time (TBT) measures the total amount of time the browser was blocked by long tasks and unable to respond to a visitor's interactions. TBT is between FCP and TTI. Tasks include things like executing JavaScript code, continuing layout and paint operations, or fetching additional resources.

Main Thread

The browser does the work involved in the critical rendering path on the main thread. The browser also responds to visitor interactions on the main thread. The main thread is single threaded, meaning that it can only complete one task at a time.

Figure 6-1 shows the main thread, represented by the horizontal line. The rectangular boxes represent three tasks on the main thread, with the rectangle width representing total task time. These tasks occurred one after another, with the first task occurring after First Contentful Paint (FCP). FCP is indicated by the vertical line.

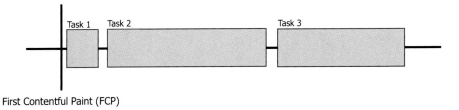

Figure 6-1. *The main thread is represented by the horizontal line. Three tasks in rectangular boxes occur after First Contentful Paint*

Defining Long Task and Task Blocking Time

Not all tasks on the main thread are equally problematic. A task that takes longer to complete will block the main thread for more time, further delaying the browser's ability to respond to a visitor's interaction. The browser can complete a shorter task quickly and that will free up the main thread faster so the browser can, in turn, respond to interactions faster. Shorter tasks can still delay the browser's ability to respond to visitor interactions, but the impact is minimal compared to the delay caused by longer tasks.

Any task on the main thread that takes longer than 50 milliseconds to complete is considered a long task.

Any task time beyond 50 milliseconds is the task's blocking time.

For example, a task that takes 200 milliseconds to complete is a long task and has 150 milliseconds of blocking time. In contrast, a task that takes 30 milliseconds to complete is a short task and has no blocking time.

Figure 6-2 updates the diagram from Figure 6-1 to show the task blocking time in the shaded area of the rectangle. Task 1 does not exceed 50 milliseconds so does not have any blocking time. Task 2 and Task 3 are long tasks, exceeding 50 milliseconds, and the shaded area shows the blocking time for each task.

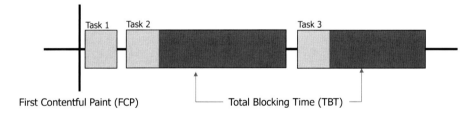

Figure 6-2. *Main thread after FCP, showing one short task and two long tasks. Blocking time is shaded on Tasks 2 and 3. Each task's blocking times are added together to calculate TBT*

TBT is the sum of all task blocking times. If Task 2's blocking time is 200 milliseconds and Task 3's blocking time is 150 milliseconds, the TBT in this example is 350 milliseconds.

Visitor Interactions When the Main Thread Is Blocked

If the visitor attempts to interact with the page when the browser is busy – or blocked– by another task, the browser will be unable to respond quickly or reliably to the visitor's interaction. In Figure 6-2, for example, if a visitor attempted to play a video when the browser was blocked by Task 2, the browser would have to delay the video play until the browser's main thread is available after Task 2 completes. Because Task 2 is a long task with a higher blocking time, this would cause the visitor to wait longer for the video to play, creating a poor user experience.

This delay often causes visitors to see a visible stutter or jerkiness – referred to as jank – in the page's design where the website appears to be unresponsive or frozen. A higher TBT or TTI means the browser will be delayed longer, causing a greater visual disruption for visitors. Lower TBT and TTI mean less delay, so there will typically be a smoother, more fluid response to visitor interactions.

When TTI Occurs

TTI occurs after the last long task. At this point, the browser's main thread is free of blocking tasks and can respond quickly to visitor interactions. There may still be short tasks running, but the main thread is not blocked long enough by the short tasks to cause noticeable disruptions.

TTI cannot be measured for real visitors and can only be measured in simulated environments by speed test tools. To calculate TTI, speed test tools need to know when the last long task has finished. This requires detecting a quiet window on the main thread. A quiet window is a period of at least 5 seconds where there are no long tasks and no more than two resource requests are in the process of loading.

Figure 6-3 shows there is a quiet window after Task 3, the last long task. Because Task 3 is the last long task before the quiet window, TTI occurs after Task 3 is completed. This means that if a visitor clicks, taps, scrolls, plays a video, fills out a form, or interacts with the page in some other way after Task 3, the browser's main thread will be available to respond quickly to an interaction. Prior to TTI, the browser would try to respond to the interaction if it could, but interactions would be delayed because of the blocking tasks on the main thread.

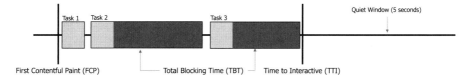

Figure 6-3. *TTI happens after the last long task before the quiet window*

If there are no long tasks after FCP, TTI happens immediately after FCP. This is because there are no long tasks blocking the main thread and the browser will be able to respond to visitor interactions immediately after the browser begins painting content.

Comparing Importance: TTI vs. TBT

TTI and TBT are complementary metrics both describing something related, but unique, about the experience visitors have interacting with the page. TBT measures how long visitors were blocked from interacting and TTI measures at what point the browser could respond quickly to visitor interactions. Both are needed to understand the experience visitors have on the website. To know which metric matters more, consider the following scenarios.

In Figure 6-4, there are four long tasks, but none have excessively long blocking times. Visitors will likely not experience a great delay if interacting during one of these tasks. As a result, TBT will be lower in this scenario. The bigger concern is the longer gaps between each task. These gaps may allow the browser more time to respond to interactions between tasks. However, with tasks stopping and starting at irregular intervals, the main thread is still active and there is no quiet window. Because of this, visitors would have to wait longer to reach the point where the browser's main thread could respond. This means TTI will be higher because it takes the browser longer to complete the last long task due to those gaps. TTI would be a more important metric to improve on this webpage to reduce the chances visitors would experience disruptions.

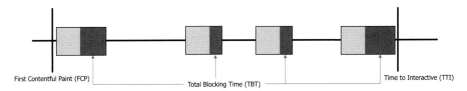

Figure 6-4. *Longer gaps between long tasks can extend TTI, even if the task block time is poor*

In Figure 6-5, two different scenarios are shown. Scenario A has three long tasks compared to one long task in Scenario B. In both scenarios, TTI will be the same and the browser will be unable to respond quickly to a visitor's interactions for the same length of time. However, TBT will be lower in Scenario A because the blocking times are spread out across three tasks instead of concentrated in a single task. In Scenario A, it is possible that the browser could respond to a visitor interaction in between one of these three tasks. Even so, TBT is still higher in both scenarios and that delays TTI. TBT would be the more important metric to optimize to improve the overall visitor experience. Reducing TBT would also reduce TTI.

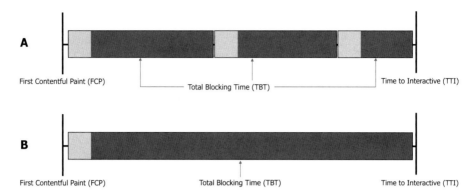

Figure 6-5. *TBT and TTI are influenced by the length of tasks and the number of tasks*

Measuring Time to Interactive and Total Blocking Time

TTI and TBT should be measured on multiple pages of the website and measured across both mobile and desktop devices. Both metrics should be measured on slower devices and on different connection speeds. The browser takes longer to complete tasks when visitors use devices with less processing power or when visitors access the website with slower connection speeds. Those differences can worsen TBT and TTI. If TBT and TTI are slower, long tasks running on the main thread can be evaluated to determine what is causing delays.

TBT and TTI Benchmarks

Google Lighthouse considers any website with a TBT below 200 milliseconds to be fast and anything over 600 milliseconds to be slow.[1] Lighthouse considers any website with a TTI below 3.8 seconds to be fast and anything over 7.3 seconds to be slow.[2]

Most websites have a slow TTI. Data from HTTP Archive shows a median TTI of 14.3 seconds on mobile websites and 4.2 seconds on desktop websites.[3] From that same data, 75% of websites have a TTI as high as 22.5 seconds on mobile websites and 6.7 seconds on desktop websites.[4]

Visualize TTI: GTmetrix Speed Visualization

Prior to TTI, visitors can see the page but cannot interact reliably with the page because other tasks block the main thread. When measuring TTI, it is helpful to understand what visitors were seeing on the page while waiting for TTI. GTmetrix's Speed Visualization report can also be used to visualize the time between when painting started (measured by FCP) and when visitors can interact with the page (measured by TTI).

After running a report in GTmetrix (`https://gtmetrix.com/`), the "Summary" tab includes the "Speed Visualization" report. Figure 6-6 shows an example, with FCP occurring at 372 milliseconds and TTI occurring at 4.5 seconds. That means a visitor on this page would have

---

[1] "Total Blocking Time." Chrome Developers. May 2, 2019, updated June 4, 2021. `https://developer.chrome.com/docs/lighthouse/performance/lighthouse-total-blocking-time/#how-lighthouse-determines-your-tbt-score`

[2] "Time to Interactive." Chrome Developers. October 9, 2019, updated June 4, 2021. `https://developer.chrome.com/docs/lighthouse/performance/interactive/#how-lighthouse-determines-your-tti-score`

[3] "Report: Loading Speed." HTTP Archive. January 1, 2024. `https://httparchive.org/reports/loading-speed#ttci`

[4] Ibid.

to wait for about 4.1 seconds between seeing the page and being able to reliably interact with the page. A visitor attempting to interact during those 4.1 seconds could experience disruptions. GTmetrix also provides TTI and TBT metrics on the "Performance" tab, shown in Figure 6-7.

Speed Visualization ?

| 3.2s | 6.4s | 9.6s |

Time to Interactive: 4.5s

First Contentful Paint: 372ms

Figure 6-6. *GTmetrix Speed Visualization*

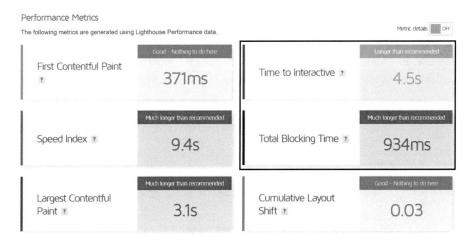

Figure 6-7. *GTmetrix Performance Metrics, including TTI and TBT*

Main Thread Processing: WebPageTest

A common recommendation for optimizing TTI or TBT is to reduce JavaScript's execution time. While that is an accurate recommendation, it does not provide specifics on what JavaScript code needs to be improved. When TBT or TTI are higher, it is important to identify what specific types of tasks are keeping the main thread busy. This clarifies what code to optimize to reduce TBT and TTI. Identifying tasks requires evaluating the main thread.

One way to evaluate the main thread is with the "Processing" reports in WebPageTest (`www.webpagetest.org/`). After running a report, in the "View" menu, select "Processing." This page contains two reports, "Processing Breakdown" and "Timing Breakdown." These breakdown reports show what specific types of events consumed the most time.

Both breakdown reports show the same data, but the "Timing Breakdown" report includes idle time. Idle time represents when the main thread was not processing any tasks. There will always be idle time, but excessive idle time can be a problem. In Figure 6-4, there was a greater amount of idle time in between tasks that delayed TTI.

The "Processing Breakdown" that excludes idle time is shown in Figure 6-8. The "Processing Categories" pie chart on the left shows how much time was spent on general processing categories:

- **Layout:** calculating the page's layout

- **Loading:** loading additional resources

- **Other:** all other types of tasks

- **Painting:** painting the page

- **Scripting:** executing JavaScript files

Processing Breakdown

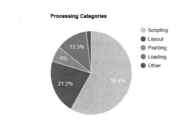

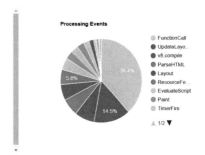

Category	Time (ms) ▼
Scripting	4,458
Layout	1,616
Loading	955
Painting	462
Other	149

Event	Time (ms) ▼
FunctionCall	2,932
UpdateLayoutTree	1,106
v8.compile	596
ParseHTML	511
Layout	475
ResourceFetcher::requestResource	444
EvaluateScript	354

Figure 6-8. *WebPageTest main thread processing report*

Scripting consumes the most processing time. This is still an overly broad category, and it is not clear which JavaScript code is being processed. However, the other processing categories clarify which JavaScript code may be a problem. In Figure 6-8, Layout consumed 21.2% or 1.6 seconds of the time. Reviewing and optimizing JavaScript functions related to page layout may help improve TTI or TBT.

For more details, the "Processing Events" section on the right of this report shows which specific events occupied the main thread. Reviewing "Processing Events" shows that 14.5%, or 1.1 seconds, of the processing time was spent updating the page layout, represented by the UpdateLayoutTree event. This event is more specific and relates to code that is adding, removing, or modifying DOM elements. This means that not only should JavaScript functions related to layout be reviewed and optimized, as suggested by "Processing Categories," but that JavaScript functions related to DOM manipulation also should be reviewed and optimized.

Find Long Tasks: Chrome DevTools

The main thread may be busy processing tasks that do not negatively affect TBT and TTI. This is because TBT and TTI are only worsened by long tasks with excessive blocking time. Optimizing those long tasks begins with finding the long tasks, which can be done using Chrome DevTools. To access Chrome DevTools, open Google Chrome and before opening a webpage, right click and choose "Inspect". Once the Chrome DevTools area opens, click "Performance" in the top bar. "Performance" may be hidden behind the ">>" icon. Once the "Performance" panel opens, click the record button, and then load the page to test.

Figure 6-9 shows a completed recording. The part to focus on is the "Main" section, indicated by the box. This shows activity on the main thread, and the individual squares and rectangles in this section indicate the various tasks running on the main thread. The report can be zoomed into by selecting a specific part of the timeline, indicated by the arrow in Figure 6-9.

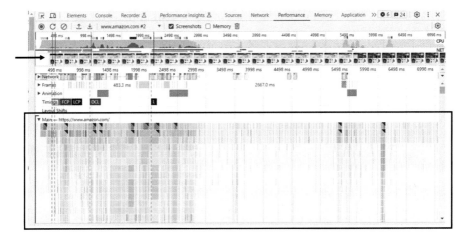

Figure 6-9. Chrome DevTools Performance Report showing Main Thread activity

Any task with a red triangle in the corner is a long task. The red striped areas represent the blocking time of the task. Hovering over a task will show what the task's time is, including the blocking time. The long task in Figure 6-10 has a total time of 64.66 milliseconds. Anything over 50 milliseconds is the blocking time so this task has a blocking time of 14.66 milliseconds.

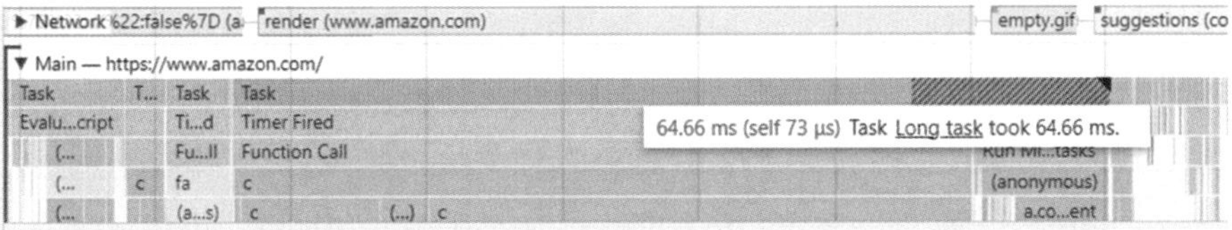

Figure 6-10. *Chrome DevTools Performance Report – zoomed in on a task – hover over a task to see the task time*

Clicking on the task will load a detailed panel summarizing the task operations, shown in Figure 6-11. The "Bottom-Up," "Call Tree," and "Event Log" tabs identify which files are involved in this task. The "Bottom-Up" tab is usually more helpful when investigating TTI or TBT because it shows which activities consumed the most time for this task. The "Event Log" tab shows tasks in the order activities occurred for this task. The "Call Tree" tab starts with root activities, or the main activities fired by the browser that initiated the JavaScript code. All three tabs will also show the details of what specific scripts are running, including the specific file name and the line of code the browser is executing. In Figure 6-11,"coupons. js:1:1132" means this task used code at character 1132 of line 1 of coupons. js. These types of details are helpful to determine what specific code needs to be optimized to speed up a long task.

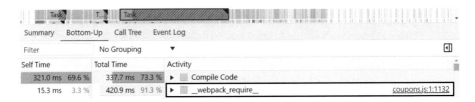

Figure 6-11. *Chrome DevTools Performance Report – task details –*
Bottom-Up tab

TTI and TBT are both affected by the speed of the visitor's connection.
To understand how different connection speeds impact task times,
network throttling can be set on the "Performance" tab, as shown in
Figure 6-12. This will simulate different network conditions. There are
default presets available or custom network throttling settings can be
defined. It is helpful to run the same page through multiple network
conditions to understand how task times change.

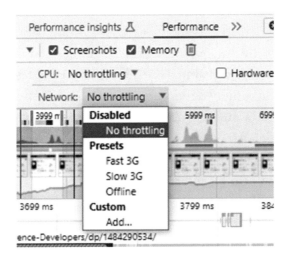

Figure 6-12. *Chrome DevTools Performance Network Throttling*

Ways to Improve Total Blocking Time and Time to Interactive

The main goal for improving TBT and TTI is to minimize long tasks running on the browser's main thread. WebPageTest's "Processing" reports and Chrome DevTools "Performance" reports will help identify specific scripts to optimize and can also identify unnecessary tasks that could be removed. Tasks that cannot be removed should be run as efficiently as possible with minimal blocking time, especially tasks involving layout and painting. Along with optimizing TBT and TTI specifically, remember that any reductions in main thread work will help improve the website's performance; the fewer tasks that are run, short or long, the less disruption there will be for visitors.

Simplify Layout Calculation and Painting: Avoid Layout Thrashing

One way to improve efficiency is to avoid problems calculating the page layout and repainting the page, both of which require extensive work on the main thread. Layout calculations and painting were discussed in Chapter 5, but one related problem was not: layout thrashing.

Layout thrashing is when JavaScript code repeatedly reads information from the DOM and then immediately writes changes to the DOM. This causes the browser to recalculate layout and repaint the page multiple times. This can create visual disruption for visitors. Thrashing can also block the main thread, preventing visitors from being able to interact with the page. As a result, layout thrashing delays TTI and worsens TBT. Batching or reducing read and write requests, can eliminate layout thrashing.

Chrome DevTools can help identify instances of layout thrashing. When reviewing the "Performance" recording, scroll through the main thread tasks and check for an excessive number of layout or recalculate activities. The report in Figure 6-13 shows an example of layout thrashing, with a repeating sequence of "Recalculate Style" and "Layout Tasks". These activities happen in rapid succession, with little time in between each sequence. This type of result means layout thrashing is occurring and needs to be addressed to improve overall website performance.

Figure 6-13. *Chrome DevTools Performance report showing layout thrashing – example generated using code from* `https://jsbin.com/ebicuJu/2/edit?js,output`

Layout thrashing differs from other types of layout problems, such as excessively long layout activity. A longer layout task is shown in Figure 6-14. The task itself is on the first row. The details of that task are on the subsequent lines, including the longer layout task on the second row. Excessively long layout tasks are not as critical as layout thrashing but are still a problem. Long layout tasks will block the main thread, potentially worsening TBT and TTI. Identifying and optimizing these tasks will help to improve performance.

Figure 6-14. *Chrome DevTools Performance report showing a longer layout task*

Move Work Off the Main Thread: Web Workers

JavaScript code can push some tasks off the main thread into a web worker. A web worker is a separate thread running in the background, parallel to the main thread. Code can pass work to a web worker to process certain tasks. Using a web worker frees up the main thread, meaning that any code running in a web worker will not contribute to TBT or TTI.

Web workers will not solve all the problems with JavaScript code. For example, a web worker is not able to directly access the DOM. Therefore, a web worker would need to send some of the work back to the main thread to make any changes to the DOM. Any processing sent back to the main thread will contribute to TBT and TTI. The goal is to keep as much of the computationally intensive work off the main thread to minimize how much JavaScript code impacts TBT and TTI.

Web workers can also be viewed in the Chrome DevTools Performance report. In Figure 6-15, the tasks running on a web worker are shown in the "Worker" section in this report which has a box around it. The worker then passes data back to the main thread for content to be displayed on the page. The tasks processed on the main thread are indicated by the arrow in this example.

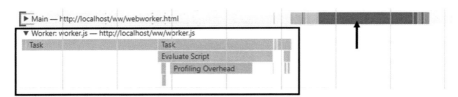

Figure 6-15. *Chrome DevTools Performance Report showing Web Worker*

111

When to Use Total Blocking Time and Time to Interactive

TTI indicates when the website is ready for visitors. This is an important step in the loading process and, as a result, TTI can be helpful to use as a KPI in reports for stakeholders.

TBT is useful to include in regular speed monitoring because changes in TBT indicate problems affecting the visitor's experience that need further investigation.

- **Is the reporting scope meaningful?** As far as visitors are concerned, once they can begin interacting with the webpage, the webpage has finished loading. While there is more work for the browser to do after TTI, TTI is one way of indicating the end of the webpage's initial load. At TTI, most of the important resources have loaded simply because most of those resources are needed for visitors to interact with the page. Because it represents an endpoint, at least for visitors, TTI is a significant event within the website loading process. TBT is more helpful for explaining why interactions might be disrupted after the browser begins painting the webpage.

- **Is it an effective business goal?** Improving TTI and TBT can help a company improve website conversion rates. For visitors to convert, they need to interact and a longer TTI or TBT delays the visitor's ability to interact. TTI is typically a clearer metric to discuss and include in stakeholder reports given the more nuanced definition of TBT. TBT, however, is often the better metric to use for monitoring performance and identifying problematic long tasks.

- **Does it describe the user experience?** TBT and TTI describe something about the user experience. Before TTI, visitors are waiting for the page to load. After TTI, visitors can begin interacting with the page. A longer TBT or TTI means the page offers a poorer user experience, forcing visitors to wait longer. The user experience might also include visual disruptions when TBT is higher. This poorer experience might be offset by other factors, like high-quality content or desirable functionality. However, improving TBT and TTI can only complement those other factors to further improve the page's quality and improve the visitor's experience.

- **How easy is it to improve?** TTI and TBT require reworking HTML, CSS, and JavaScript code so that code can load more efficiently with less blocking time. JavaScript code affects TTI and TBT the most, especially when there are problems like layout thrashing. Unfortunately, JavaScript code is rarely easy to improve and problems like layout thrashing can be bigger undertakings. TBT or TTI are even harder to address if they are worsened because of third-party resources that are outside of the organization's control. In these cases, there may be opportunities to adjust how code is loaded, such as minifying code or using *async* and *defer*, to improve efficiencies in the main thread work.

- **How impactful are improvements?** Any improvements in TTI and TBT are often highly impactful. Interacting a few hundred milliseconds quicker can make the website feel that much faster. This change in perception provides a competitive advantage. TBT is often the more impactful of the two because any reductions in blocking time reduce visual disruptions that frustrate visitors. With an improved TBT, interactions with the page will feel smoother and more fluid, resulting in a better user experience. Reducing TBT can also improve later-stage speed metrics, especially metrics describing the user experience.

CHAPTER 7

Total Load: Onload Time, Fully Loaded Time, Speed Index

The question "when is the website done loading?" seems like it should have a simple answer. Ultimately though, webpages are never truly done loading. As visitors interact with a page, more resources may need to be loaded, more code may need to be executed, or the browser may need to repaint portions of the page to display new content. Yet, there are points at which the page has completed key aspects of the initial load. At these points, visitors can begin using and interacting with different parts of the webpage.

What Do Onload Time, Fully Loaded Time, and Speed Index Measure

Onload (or load) is an event triggered in the browser when the page's dependent resources have loaded. **Onload Time** is when the onload event occurs.

Fully Loaded Time measures when the website has finished loading all files, not just dependent resources. It is measured by waiting for some amount of network idle time after Onload Time.

Speed Index is a calculation measuring how quickly the webpage became visually complete.

Onload Time and Dependent Resources

The onload event is triggered, or fired, when all dependent resources have loaded. Dependent resources are any files referenced directly in the page's HTML code. For example, if an HTML page links to a stylesheet, that stylesheet is a dependent resource and will be loaded before the onload event.

There are other types of files loaded that are not referenced directly in the HTML. The stylesheet may reference a font file via a *@font-face* declaration, but that font file is not referenced in the main HTML document. In this case, the font file would not be considered a dependent resource of the HTML page. The loading of that font file would not affect the onload event and may load after Onload Time.

There are some dependent resources that may not load before the onload event. An image or iframe using lazy load will not load before the onload event. As discussed in Chapter 5, lazy load means these elements will only load once the visitor scrolls to where they are located on the page. The visitor may not scroll before the onload event fires.

Fully Loaded Time and Network Idle Time

There can still be network activity after the onload event fires because of the additional files loaded by the page's dependent resources. Even after Onload Time, images, fonts, videos, and other files referenced by the HTML page's dependent resources still need to be loaded. Fully Loaded Time measures how long it takes to load these additional files. Once those files load, there is a period of network idle time where the browser is no longer fetching resources from the server and the server is no longer transferring data to the browser.

Fully Loaded Time is a lab metric, measured in speed testing tools. These tools will wait for some period of network idle time, usually a few seconds, before considering the page fully loaded. Each tool defines Fully Loaded Time somewhat differently. For example, GTmetrix's Fully Loaded Time measures the time after First Contentful Paint and the onload event have occurred, plus 5.25 seconds of network idle time. Because it is not measured until a period of network idle time, Fully Loaded Time better reflects when the browser has finished loading all the files it needs to finish loading the page. This can make Fully Loaded Time a more accurate measure of a webpage's total loading time than Onload Time.

On resource-intensive websites, Fully Loaded Time may be quite high as it takes longer for all files to load until there is a period of network idle time. Even though additional files might be loading, the webpage may still be complete enough for visitors to interact with the website even though Fully Loaded Time has not yet occurred.

This relates to Time to Interactive and Total Blocking Time, discussed in Chapter 6. Those metrics measure the amount of main thread activity, which includes fetching additional files. If the goal is to measure how long it takes for all the page's associated files to load, Fully Loaded Time is the better metric to use. Time to Interactive or Total Blocking Time are better metrics to use when the goal is understanding how quickly visitors can interact with the page.

Speed Index and Visually Complete

Measuring when the website is visually complete is a different way of determining when a webpage has finished loading. Visually Complete time is when there are no more visual changes detected on the page. At Visually Complete time, it appears to a visitor that all elements are present on the page.

Speed Index does not measure when the page is visually complete. Instead, Speed Index measures how visually complete the page was at different slices of time during the page load. Once the page is visually complete, the visual completion percentage at each slice of time is added together. A smaller total number means there are fewer time slices to add up because the page appeared faster for visitors. A larger number means there are more time slices to add up because the page appeared slower for visitors.

In Figure 7-1, the page was visually complete in 15 seconds. Some of the visual parts of the page loaded relatively quickly, with 68% of the page available within 4 seconds. Other visual content loaded more slowly, given that the page did not reach 100% visual completion until 15 seconds. Speed Index's calculation balances out these faster and slower portions of the visual load. In this example, the Speed Index for this page is only 6.088 seconds. This means that 6.088 seconds of the total load time was spent loading the visual parts of the page. This gives a sense of how long visitors had to stare at a blank white screen while waiting for this page to load.

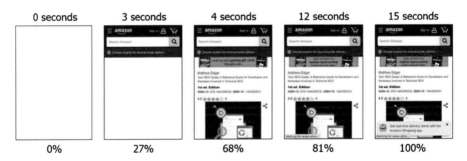

Figure 7-1. *Filmstrip view of a website with a 6.088 second Speed Index and a 15 second Visually Complete time, measured by WebPageTest*

To understand how Speed Index and Visually Complete time compare, consider the website loaded in Figure 7-1 with the website loaded in Figure 7-2. The webpage in Figure 7-2 reaches visual completion faster than the webpage in Figure 7-1 by a full second. However, visitors to the webpage in Figure 7-2 spend more time staring at a blank screen. This longer wait time is reflected in a slower Speed Index of 12.375 seconds.

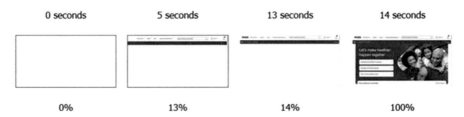

Figure 7-2. *Filmstrip view of a website with a 14 second Visually Complete time and a 12.375 second Speed Index, measured by WebPageTest*

To make the difference clear, Figure 7-3 compares these two webpages in a "Visual Progress" graph. The graph shows how Amazon's website, shown in Figure 7-1, made visual progress more quickly during the load time. It also had more visual progress events – the graph steps up slightly at various intervals during the website load. In contrast, CVS's website, shown in Figure 7-2, has fewer visual progress events and remains a flat line for longer until a large jump at the end. The reports shown in these figures are described in more detail later in this chapter.

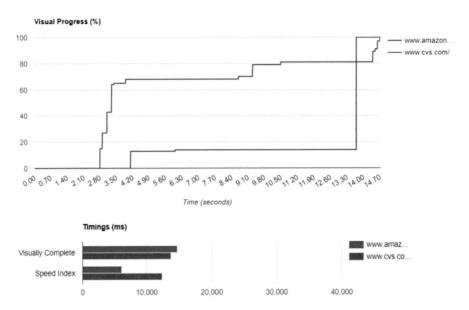

Figure 7-3. *Comparing Visually Complete time and Speed Index times in WebPageTest. A faster Visually Complete time does not mean a faster Speed Index. Note: The Timings graph is edited to only show Visually Complete and Speed Index*

Determining When the Website Finishes Loading

Onload Time, Fully Loaded Time, and Speed Index each capture a different idea of when a webpage has finished loading. In addition, each metric offers unique insight into what kind of experience visitors had waiting for the page to load.

- Onload Time measures when the page's dependent files have loaded. This is helpful to know when files referenced in the webpage's HTML code have been processed by the browser. A longer Onload Time suggests the visitor waited a longer time for those files to load, potentially delaying their ability to use or see the page. However, other types of files may load after the onload event fires and the loading of those files is not captured by Onload Time.

- Fully Loaded Time attempts to work around the problems with Onload Time by monitoring for network idle time once all files have loaded. Fully Loaded Time may not accurately reflect when the page is ready for visitors because some of the files loaded after onload may not be critical for how visitors use the page.

- Speed Index answers a different but related question: how quickly can visitors see the page? Onload or Fully Loaded Time can happen after the page is visually complete as more resources are loaded. Speed Index gives a sense of when visitors would feel like the page is ready. Unlike Visually Complete time, Speed Index focuses on visual progress during the website load instead of measuring when painting finishes.

Time to Interactive, discussed in Chapter 6, is another way of measuring when the website has finished loading. It focuses on when the page is ready to reliably respond to visitor interactions. A longer Time to Interactive means visitors waited longer before they could interact with the page. However, at Time to Interactive, there could still be smaller files loading that do not create long tasks and some paint operations may still be in progress to finish displaying the page.

Understanding the total load time of a given webpage requires measuring a combination of metrics. No one metric can fully define the complex process of completing the initial website load. Instead, it is best to select the most meaningful combination of metrics, given each website's unique nature to reflect the point in time when the initial load has completed enough for visitors.

Measuring Total Load Metrics

Onload Time, Fully Loaded Time, and Speed Index should be measured on multiple pages to understand the different total load time ranges that exist on the website. To better understand the range of Onload and Fully Loaded Times across the website, pages with varying amounts of resource files should be evaluated. To better understand the range of Speed Index across the website, pages of varying visual complexity should be tested. These metrics should also be tested on different device types with different connection speeds because slower devices will take longer to display the webpage and finish loading all resources.

Onload Time Benchmarks

There is no official benchmark for Onload Time. According to HTTP Archive, the median mobile website's onload time is 10.6 seconds and the median desktop website's onload time is 6.5 seconds.[1]

Fully Loaded Time Benchmarks

No official benchmarks or reliable median data exist for Fully Loaded Time. If used regularly, Fully Loaded Time should be measured and benchmarked on a per website, or per webpage, basis.

---

[1] "Report: Loading Speed." HTTP Archive. October 1, 2023. https://httparchive.org/reports/loading-speed

Speed Index Benchmarks

Google's Lighthouse report considers a Speed Index under 3.4 seconds to be fast and anything over 5.8 seconds to be slow.[2] According to data from HTTP Archive, the median mobile website's Speed Index is 6.5 seconds and the median desktop website's Speed Index is 4.3 seconds.[3]

Onload and Fully Loaded Time: GTmetrix

The "Speed Visualization" timeline shown in GTmetrix (`https://gtmetrix.com/`), discussed in Chapters 5 and 6, will also show the Onload Time and the Fully Loaded Time. This is helpful to see where these metrics are in relation to First Contentful Paint and Time to Interactive. In Figure 7-4, Onload Time occurs shortly after Time to Interactive. However, more resources are loaded after Time to Interactive and Onload Time, keeping the browser busy. This pushes Fully Loaded Time out to 14.6 seconds, 10.3 seconds after Onload Time.

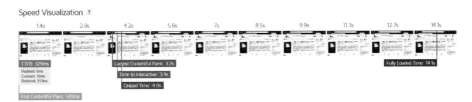

Figure 7-4. *GTmetrix Speed Visualization*

---

[2] "Speed Index." 2019. Chrome for Developers. Google for Developers. May 2, 2019. `https://developer.chrome.com/en/docs/lighthouse/performance/speed-index/#how-lighthouse-determines-your-speed-index-score`

[3] "Report: Loading Speed." HTTP Archive. October 1, 2023. `https://httparchive.org/reports/loading-speed`

GTmetrix also provides a "Waterfall Chart" showing which files were loaded at specific times, with those key times indicated by vertical lines. This helps to identify what files are contributing to longer delays in reaching Onload or Fully Loaded Times. Loading those files faster improves the total page load. To access the chart, click the "Waterfall" tab after running a report.

In Figure 7-5, the "Waterfall Chart" is scrolled to the end of the list of resources to show the last files that were loaded. Vertical lines indicate key timing events, including the Onload Time and the Fully Loaded Time. The vertical line representing the Fully Loaded Time is pushed out by the resources that have their horizontal bars touching that line. This chart also shows the domain and size for each resource file. Domain information will identify if these are third-party or self-hosted resources. Optimizing larger files will have a greater impact.

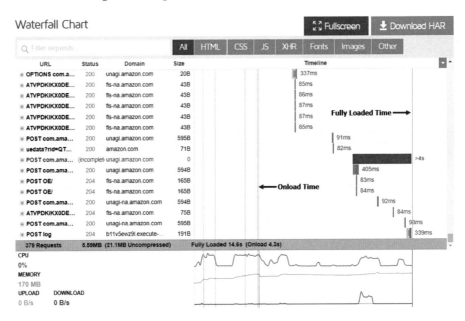

Figure 7-5. *Bottom of GTmetrix Waterfall Report, with Onload Time and Fully Loaded Time represented by vertical lines*

GTmetrix's "Waterfall" report also includes a "Resource Usage Graph," as seen at the bottom of Figure 7-5. This shows CPU usage, memory usage, and bandwidth usage (labeled as Upload and Download). This graph indicates how busy the browser was when loading this webpage's files. The busier the browser, the more delays visitors may experience when trying to use the page and the longer it will take for the website to finish loading.

Hovering over different parts of the graph will show what resources were being used at a specific time interval. GTmetrix includes the vertical lines in the "Resource Usage Graph" to show key load times. For example, Figure 7-6 shows the resource usage at a time approximately halfway between Onload Time and Fully Loaded Time. The selected time is marked by the light gray vertical line, indicated by the arrow in this figure. The time selected for this example happens to be one of the lower points for CPU usage, with CPU usage only at 7.1%. The browser was not executing much code at this time. However, other stages in between Onload and Fully Loaded Times are more active, as can be seen by the peaks and valleys in the lines on this graph. Review which files were loading at this time in the "Waterfall" chart to determine what files caused the biggest peaks in resource usage.

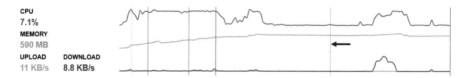

Figure 7-6. *GTmetrix resource usage graph*

Speed Index and Visual Progress: WebPageTest

Speed Index is reported on the "Performance Summary" report in WebPageTest (`www.webpagetest.org/`). To better understand Speed Index, WebPageTest offers a detailed filmstrip report showing the progression of how the website visually loaded. Portions of that filmstrip were shown in Figures 1 and 2. This report also includes the "Visual Progress" graph shown in Figure 7-3.

To access these reports, select "Filmstrip" from the "View" menu after running a test. The filmstrip shows the visual progression as the webpage was loaded. The percentage shows the amount of the page that was visually complete at the time interval marked above the image. The filmstrip is layered on top of a waterfall chart of all loaded resources. Scrolling left or right in the filmstrip will show which resources were loading at that time. In Figure 7-7, the filmstrip is at the 3-second mark with 27% of the page loaded. The indicator line on the waterfall, noted by the arrow in this figure, shows what files were loading at this 3-second mark. This helps identify which files may be delaying the visual presentation of the page. As with all tests run through WebPageTest, this can be run from different locations and on different device types to see how the visitor's geographic location or device type changes the visual presentation of the page.

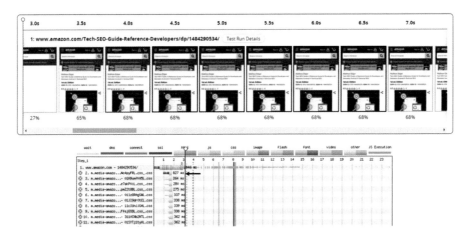

Figure 7-7. *Filmstrip View report in WebPageTest*

Below the filmstrip and waterfall, WebPageTest also presents the "Visual Progress" graph, shown in Figure 7-8. This graph makes it easier to identify precisely what percentage of the page was displayed at various intervals through the website load. It also shows how active the browser was in painting page elements. Each step up in the graph reflects something being painted. If there are many painting events, like Amazon's website in the example shown in Figure 7-3, that means continual progress is being made painting elements. Visitors would see elements being actively painted, possibly making the website feel faster. Flat lines on the graph, like those seen in Figure 7-8, represent time when nothing was painted. During these times, visitors might think the webpage is broken or has stalled.

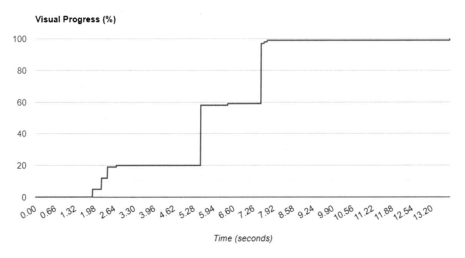

Figure 7-8. *WebPageTest Visual Progress graph*

The "Filmstrip" report also provides a "Timings" graph showing how key speed metrics compare. This can be helpful in determining which metric has the biggest opportunity. The graph, shown in Figure 7-9, includes Speed Index and Visually Complete times. It also includes the time of the Last Visual Change and the time certain Visually Complete percentages were reached. Onload and Fully Loaded times are also reported.

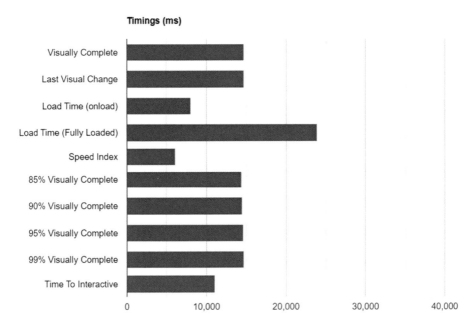

Figure 7-9. *WebPageTest – Timings graph on the Filmstrip report. Note: The graph presented has been edited to only highlight metrics relevant to this chapter. The full graph includes additional metrics*

Ways to Improve Total Load Time

Onload Time, Fully Loaded Time, and Speed Index represent the end of the initial webpage load. As a result, they are not directly actionable. Instead, optimizing these metrics requires addressing issues in earlier stages of the webpage's loading process. Slower speeds during the initial connection or the critical render path will delay the total load. When these metrics are higher, the first step is to review earlier-stage metrics to understand what is causing the webpage to load slowly. Higher Onload and Fully Loaded Times often indicate problems with loading the HTML, discussed in Chapter 3, and loading resources, discussed in Chapter 4. Speed Index is typically interconnected with how the page is painted, so paint-related metrics like First Contentful Paint will often be higher when Speed Index is higher. If these earlier stages cannot be addressed and total load times cannot be improved, there may be ways to improve the perception of speed.

Progress Indicators Improve Perception of Speed

Longer total load times mean longer waiting times. To offset longer waiting times, progress indicators can be used to make it appear that something is happening. This way visitors do not have to look at a blank white screen and wonder if the website is working. The slower the page, the more some type of progress indicator is needed. Different types of indicators can be used, including progress bars, progress circles, spinners, animated graphics, text messages, or skeleton screens. Three broad questions can help determine which type is appropriate.

1. Should the progress indicator be used for the whole page or certain elements on the page? A progress indicator could be used for the entire page, such as a spinning circle on an otherwise blank screen to let visitors know loading is in progress. If only certain elements on a page take longer to load, a progress indicator could be used for just that element. For example, a blank space could be provided where a video will eventually appear, and a spinner could be used in that space while waiting for the video to load.

2. Should the progress indicator be determinate or indeterminate? A determinate progress indicator says specifically what is loading and how much progress is being made. This is helpful for longer wait times. For example, visitors may want to know

the progress of a form submission, so a loading bar could increase incrementally as each step of the submission is completed. A percentage could be shown alongside those indicators to communicate more details about the loading process. Indeterminate indicators do not provide details and are better suited for shorter wait times. For example, a simple spinner or "loading..." message could be shown for a few seconds while a larger image loads.

3. How much visual detail needs to be provided? Indicators like spinners or progress bars can give some indication that activity is occurring, but they typically sit on a blank white screen. This does not provide much detail for visitors about what will be loaded. However, when the whole page is slow, showing more visual details might ease visitor frustration. Skeleton or stencil screens, like YouTube's shown in Figure 7-10, offer more details about what will eventually appear.

Figure 7-10. *YouTube's skeleton, or stencil, screen*

Recap: When to Use Total Load Metrics

Onload Time and Fully Loaded Time are best used on an as-needed basis to explain the duration of the entire website load.

Speed Index is best used either as part of regular monitoring or as a speed KPI to describe the experience visitors had watching the website load.

- **Is the reporting scope meaningful?** Onload and Fully Loaded Time are broad metrics, encompassing the entirety of the website's initial load. This broad scope makes these metrics less helpful when trying to diagnose why a website is slow. Other metrics are better for determining what causes delays. Speed Index focuses on visual completeness, so its scope is narrower than Onload Time or Fully Loaded Time. This makes it a more useful metric because if Speed Index is slower, it is clearer what types of problems exist.

- **Is it an effective business goal?** Some organizations use Onload Time or Fully Loaded Time as KPIs to give a general sense of how long it takes the website to load. These might be easier metrics to share with a wider group of stakeholders. It is not always clear how Onload or Fully Loaded Time relate to conversion or engagement rates because visitors may be able to see the page and interact with the page before Onload Time or Fully Loaded Time. Speed Index can be helpful to use as a KPI – if a page appears faster, visitors can convert or engage faster.

- **Does it describe the user experience?** Speed Index describes an important aspect of the experience visitors have on the website: how long does the website take to visually appear? Websites that appear faster will feel faster, even if there is a longer Onload Time or Fully Loaded Time. Onload Time and Fully Loaded Time do not say much about the experience visitors have. Indirectly, these metrics indicate how busy the browser is when loading the webpage. The busier the browser is, the less responsive the browser will be for visitors. Time to Interactive and Total Blocking Time offer better ways of measuring the browser's responsiveness to show how delays affect visitors.

- **How easy is it to improve?** Onload Time and Fully Loaded Time are easier to improve simply because they can be improved by almost any speed optimization tactic. Any change in earlier stage metrics will improve Onload Time or Fully Loaded Time. Speed Index is somewhat harder to improve because it requires addressing how items are painted. It is easier to improve Speed Index than other paint-related metrics because any improvements in how elements are painted will help improve Speed Index – a website could have a slow First Paint but have an acceptable Speed Index.

- **How impactful are improvements?** Because Onload Time and Fully Loaded Time are so broad, any impacts on the user experience or on business goals are indirect. These metrics are only improved when other metrics are improved. If Onload Time or Fully Loaded Time cannot be improved, slower speeds can be offset by progress indicators to improve the perception of speed. Improvements in Speed Index typically indicate improvements in other paint-related metrics. Also, improvements in Speed Index can have a notable impact on the user experience because visitors will see the webpage faster.

PART IV

Core Web Vitals

CHAPTER 8

Largest Contentful Paint

Visitors are not waiting for just any content to load on the webpage. The browser may quickly load and paint the webpage's supplementary content, such as the website's header navigation, but this content will not satisfy visitors. If visitors are loading a product page on an ecommerce website, they want to see information about that product. If visitors are loading an article on a news website, they want to read that article's text. If visitors have come to a page to complete a form, then visitors want to interact with that form. In short, visitors are waiting for the webpage's main content to load. The faster the browser paints the webpage's main content, the more satisfying the visitor experience. Typically, the webpage's main content will also be the webpage's largest content.

What Largest Contentful Paint Measures

Largest Contentful Paint (LCP) is a Core Web Vitals metric that measures the time when the webpage's largest content element is painted in the visitor's first viewport.

© Matthew Edgar 2024
M. Edgar, *Speed Metrics Guide*, https://doi.org/10.1007/979-8-8688-0155-6_8

Viewport and First Viewport

The viewport is the visible area of the website shown on the visitor's device. The first viewport is the first visible section of the website visitors see. The content in a mobile device's first viewport will differ from a desktop device's first viewport. Regardless of the device, visitors expect to see the elements contained in this first viewport load quickly. LCP measures how well the website meets that expectation by measuring when the largest content element contained in the first viewport is painted.

Defining "Largest"

To measure when the largest element is painted, the browser needs to know what element is the largest. Largest does not refer to the file's byte size. Instead, an element is considered the largest based on the overall area the element occupies in the viewport. The largest element is referred to as the LCP element. When the LCP element is painted, LCP occurs.

For example, Figure 8-1 shows a webpage's first viewport with three elements: an image at the top of the viewport, a paragraph of text, and the start of another image at the bottom of the viewport. In this example, the text element occupies the most space and is the LCP element. The browser evaluates the size of a text element based on the dimensions of the smallest rectangle that contains all the text visible in the viewport. If the dimensions of that rectangle make the text element the largest element in the viewport, as is the case in the example shown in Figure 8-1, then LCP would measure the time when that text element is painted.

Figure 8-1. *Wireframe of website showing three painted elements. The LCP element is the paragraph because it occupies the most area in the viewport*

Images have two sizes to consider: visible size and intrinsic size. The visible size is the width and height of the element as it is painted. The intrinsic size is the original width and height of the element. Google will use whichever size is smaller to determine what element is largest when measuring LCP for Core Web Vitals. For example, an image may have an intrinsic size of 500x500 pixels but scale to a visible size of 100x100 pixels, so the visible size of 100x100 pixels would be used when evaluating LCP.

In the context of LCP, the element's size does not include any margin, padding, or borders around that element. LCP will also not consider the portions of any element that extends outside the visitor's first viewport or any portions of the element that are hidden from view. In Figure 8-1, only a portion of the image at the bottom of the screen is shown. So, when determining what the LCP element is, only the image's size visible in the viewport would be considered. The goal with LCP is to measure how long it takes for the largest content visitors can see in the page's first viewport to be painted. The time it takes to paint any non-content aspects of the element or any aspects of the element not visible in the first viewport are irrelevant.

How LCP Compares to FCP

First Contentful Paint (FCP) is a measurement of painting order, answering the question: what element was painted first? In contrast, LCP is not concerned with the order an item is painted and, instead, focuses on the element's size in the viewport. LCP answers the question: when is the largest element painted? As a result, these metrics communicate different aspects of painting. It is possible, though unlikely, that the first element painted might also be the largest element painted.

This difference exists because LCP is trying to measure something more meaningful than FCP. This can also be seen in how LCP has a stricter definition for content than FCP. As discussed in Chapter 5, FCP uses a broad definition of content, essentially looking for the first thing painted on the page. For example, a background image or a loading icon might be the first element painted. FCP is an important indicator of a website's early loading stages, but the content painted first is typically not the content visitors want to see or engage with on the page. Visitors want to see and engage with the webpage's main content.

To account for this, LCP, unlike FCP, narrows the definition to capture elements that are more likely to be the website's main content. Content considered by LCP includes the following:

- Images, including SVG images, background images, and the first frame of an animated image

- Videos, either measuring the poster image or the first frame of an autoplay video

- Block level elements containing text, like a paragraph or heading

Elements that are less likely to contain main content are removed from consideration:

- Elements hidden from view

- Images that cover the full viewport, which are considered background instead of main content

- Low-entropy images, or low-content images, like images containing a single color

When LCP Occurs

The largest element on a page, or the LCP element, can change as more files are loaded and more elements are painted. In Figure 8-2, an image is the first element loaded and painted at the 1.0 second mark. Initially, this image would be the LCP element. At the 1.5 second mark, a text block is painted, and that text block is larger than the image. So, the text block is now the LCP element, and LCP is updated to reflect the time this element was painted. At the 2.0 second mark, another image is painted. However, this element does not consume much area in the first viewport and would not be considered the LCP element and LCP would remain 1.5 seconds.

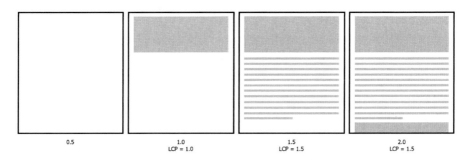

Figure 8-2. *Timeline of when elements are painted on a wireframe website*

Because of this continual updating, the LCP element may end up outside the first viewport, even though LCP attempts to only evaluate the first viewport visitors see. This happens because LCP measures the original position of the elements in the viewport as elements are painted. If a large image initially loads in the first viewport but is pushed down outside the first viewport during the webpage's loading, that image still can be the LCP element.

The continual updating of LCP also means removed content elements can be the LCP element. For example, an image might be initially painted as part of an image carousel. When it is loaded, that image would be the LCP element and LCP would reflect the time that image was painted. However, the image would be removed from the page as the carousel rotates through subsequent images. The subsequent images may not be as large as that first image, so LCP would still reflect the time that first image was painted.

The browser will continue updating LCP as new elements are painted, until the visitor begins scrolling or interacting with the page. While the largest element can also change as visitors interact with the page or scroll down the page, those changes will not be reflected in the page's LCP.

Measuring Largest Contentful Paint

Each page of the website had different content and will have a different LCP element. As a result, LCP should be measured across different pages of the website. Templated pages often have the same LCP element. For example, a blog post template may use a header image above the text. While the header image itself will change on each blog post, the header image is likely to be the LCP element for all blog posts using that template. If templates are used, begin measuring LCP across the main template types to identify common LCP elements. It is also important to measure LCP across different connection speeds and device types to determine where there might be a problem. An LCP element may load quickly on the latest smartphone model using a WiFi connection but will load slower on a three-year old smartphone using mobile data.

LCP Benchmarks

According to Google's Core Web Vitals guidelines, LCP should be within 2.5 seconds and an LCP greater than 4 seconds is considered slow.[1] According to HTTP Archive's data assessing millions of websites, 68.8% of desktop websites meet this threshold, but only 54.9% of mobile websites do.[2]

Identify LCP Element: WebPageTest

The first step is to identify the LCP element. WebPageTest (*www. webpagetest.org/*) offers a report showing what the LCP element is and details about how that element loads. After running a test, select "Web Vitals" from the "View" menu and scroll to the LCP section of the report. The example in Figure 8-3 shows an H1 tag as the LCP element in the "Element Type" row and shows the element in the HTML code in the "Outer HTML" row. WebPageTest shows the element's size in square pixels, 41,005 px^2 in this example, and the time this element loaded, 3,657 milliseconds.

---

[1] McQuade, Bryan. 2022. "Defining the Core Web Vitals Metrics Thresholds." Web.dev. July 18, 2022. https://web.dev/articles/defining-core-web-vitals-thresholds

[2] "Report: CrUX." HTTP Archive. October 1, 2023. https://httparchive.org/reports/chrome-ux-report#cruxFastLcp

Largest Contentful Paint (3657 ms)

View as Filmstrip - View Video - About Largest Contentful Paint (LCP)

LCP Event Summary

See full details

Time	3657ms
Size	41005px²
Type	text
Element Type	H1
Outer HTML	`<h1 class="fxg-title fxg-supscript">Select Your Location and Language</h1>...`

Figure 8-3. *WebPageTest Web Vitals report, showing an H1 as the LCP element*

A waterfall chart is provided on this page and shows all the elements that loaded up to when LCP occurs. This chart shows when any non-text LCP elements loaded. In Figure 8-4, an image is the LCP element and is shown on line 5 of the waterfall. The waterfall shows this file began loading 0.7 seconds into the webpage's load and finished loading shortly before the 1.2-second mark. This results in 474 milliseconds of total loading time for the image. However, LCP does not occur until 1.788 seconds as reported by the "LCP Event Summary" table. This makes it clear there is a delay between when this webpage loads and when the LCP element is painted. LCP is at an acceptable level on this page, but there could be an opportunity to improve LCP further by reducing the delay. Alternatively, the LCP element could be loaded before the files shown on lines 2, 3, and 4 of the waterfall chart. This would allow the image to start loading sooner than 0.7 seconds into the page's load time, potentially painting faster as well.

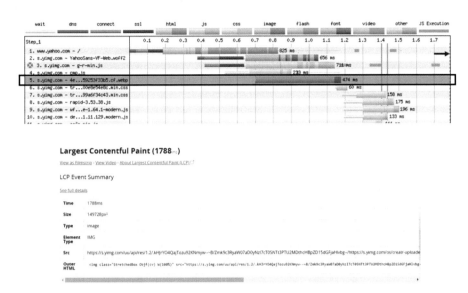

Figure 8-4. *WebPageTest Web Vitals report waterfall chart, showing all elements that loaded before LCP occurred. The LCP element is indicated by the box. The arrow indicates when LCP occurs*

Measuring Visitor Viewport Size: GA4

When evaluating LCP, it is important to determine what content will appear for most visitors in the first viewport. This requires knowing what the common viewports are for visitors and reviewing what content is likely to appear within that viewport. By reviewing the viewport, decisions can be made about what content may not be needed, or at least not needed within the first viewport. Removing larger content elements or moving those elements lower on the page can help improve LCP.

Many web analytics tools, like GA4, only measure screen resolution by default and not the viewport size. Screen resolution reflects the full physical dimensions of the visitor's device. The screen resolution includes space for the interface elements – like the address bar or system status bar. After accounting for those elements, a smaller part of the screen, the viewport, is available to view the website.

145

While the viewport size is not available by default, it can be measured in GA4 using a custom dimension. A JavaScript function can get the viewport size and send it to GA4 through a Google Tag Manager variable. Figure 8-5 shows an example of a custom JavaScript function getting the viewport size, storing this size as a variable, and then sending this variable to GA4 as a custom dimension within the main GA4 configuration tag. Figure 8-6 shows an example GA4 Exploration generated using this custom dimension.

Figure 8-5. *Viewport size defined as a custom JavaScript variable in Google Tag Manager for GA4, from* www.matthewedgar.net/google-analytics-viewport-or-browser-size/

Free form 1 ▾ +	↺ ⤳ ↓ ➕ ⊘
visitor_viewport	↓ Total users
5 1536x739	86
6 1536x707	79
7 1366x651	75
8 1536x715	71
9 1536x747	57
10 1366x619	49

Figure 8-6. *Example viewport size report in GA4*

After collecting this information, the next step is determining what the largest content element is within each viewport size. The viewport size can be emulated in a variety of tools, including Chrome's DevTools. Before opening a webpage in Chrome, open Chrome DevTools by right-clicking and selecting "Inspect".

Once DevTools opens, select the "Device Mode" icon, shown in the upper left corner of Figure 8-7. After "Device Mode" opens, select "Responsive" and specify the different viewport sizes used by website visitors. Figure 8-7 shows the viewport set to a size of 1536x739. Once the viewport dimensions are set, load the webpage. After it loads, note which elements are viewable in the first viewport and find these elements in the waterfall report from WebPageTest to determine how quickly each is loaded.

Figure 8-7. *Responsive Design in Chrome DevTools*

Ways to Improve Largest Contentful Paint

The LCP element should be one of the first items loaded. The quicker the LCP element loads, the faster the browser will be able to paint that element. If the element itself cannot be loaded sooner, adjusting the priority of the element can help the browser load and paint the LCP element faster. Along with adjusting priority, the LCP element needs to be optimized to load quickly. For example, if the LCP element is an image, there may be opportunities to improve LCP by changing the image's format.

Preload LCP Elements

The waterfall report from WebPageTest helps identify when the LCP item loads and if there are opportunities to load the LCP element earlier. In Figure 8-4, the LCP element was the fifth item loaded. While there may be some opportunity for improvement by loading that element second or third, fifth is still relatively early in the website's load and LCP was not a problem for that website.

In contrast, consider the waterfall in Figure 8-8 where the LCP element is an image that is the eleventh file loaded. Fonts, JavaScript, and CSS files are all loaded before this image. This results in the LCP element not starting to load until five seconds have already elapsed. Even if this image were able to load instantaneously, five seconds is already above the LCP benchmark of 2.5 seconds. Of course, this image does not load instantaneously, instead taking 1.52 seconds to load. To meet the 2.5 second benchmark, this element would need to start loading no more than one second into the page's load.

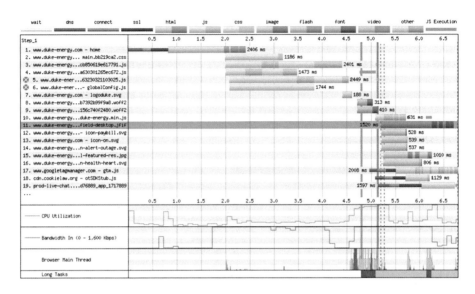

Figure 8-8. *WebPageTest waterfall showing an LCP element as the eleventh loaded element*

To help correct problems like the one shown in Figure 8-8, the image could be referenced in a *preload* tag. As discussed in Chapter 4, preloaded elements are given a high fetch priority, resulting in a faster loading time for that element. The *preload* tag is added to the page's HTML head and shown in this example:

```
<link rel="preload" as="image" href="https://www.site.com/a.JPEG">
```

The impact of the *preload* tag can be evaluated using WebPageTest's experiment feature. The experiment feature is only available for paying users. While a paid tool, this is an effective way to evaluate if changes will help before investing in development resources. In the "View" menu, select "Opportunities & Experiments". Recommended experiments are listed in this report as opportunities or custom experiments can be defined. After selecting a recommended experiment or defining a custom experiment, WebPageTest will re-run the test and compare the page with the changes to a control version without those changes.

The results of the experiment are shown in Figure 8-9, with the *preload* tag reducing LCP by half a second and reducing LCP from 6.92 seconds to 6.41 seconds. While this would not bring this page's LCP within the 2.5 second threshold, using a *preload* tag would be an important part of reducing LCP.

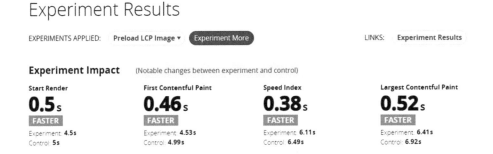

Figure 8-9. *WebPageTest Experiment Results – Add a preload tag for an LCP Image*

Another related way of encouraging the browser to load the LCP image faster is with *fetchpriority*. As discussed in Chapter 4, the *fetchpriority* attribute can be added to an element to give the browser a hint that the element should move up the priority order. Changes to *fetchpriority* can also be tested in WebPageTest's Experiment feature with the results shown in Figure 8-10. In this case, using *fetchpriority* improved LCP by 1.13 seconds, reducing LCP from 7.74 seconds in the control to 6.61 seconds.

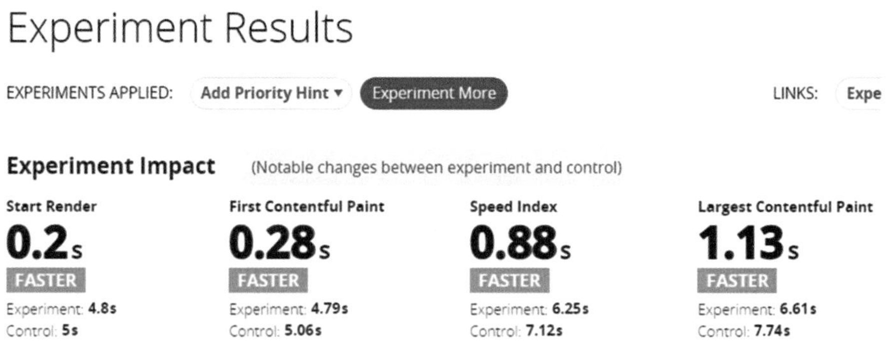

Experiment Results

EXPERIMENTS APPLIED: **Add Priority Hint ▾**   **Experiment More**   LINKS: **Expe**

Experiment Impact   (Notable changes between experiment and control)

Start Render	First Contentful Paint	Speed Index	Largest Contentful Paint
0.2s	**0.28**s	**0.88**s	**1.13**s
FASTER	FASTER	FASTER	FASTER
Experiment: 4.8s	Experiment: 4.79s	Experiment: 6.25s	Experiment: 6.61s
Control: 5s	Control: 5.06s	Control: 7.12s	Control: 7.74s

Figure 8-10. *WebPageTest Experiment Results – Add fetchpriority attribute to LCP image*

When the LCP element is a text block, a *preload* tag can improve LCP by preloading resource files that delay the text block's painting. For example, a JavaScript file might detect where the visitor is located and generate custom text based on that location. The associated text would not be painted until that JavaScript file executes, making the text's painting dependent on when the JavaScript file is loaded and executed by the browser. In this situation, using *preload* for the JavaScript file would give that file greater priority so that the browser would load and execute the file more quickly. If that JavaScript file is loaded and executed more quickly, then the associated text will also paint more quickly. Painting the text more quickly would improve LCP.

More often though, text elements are delayed because of font files used to style that text. As discussed in prior chapters, fonts are loaded synchronously by default, and this will hide the text from view until the font files are ready. Using a system font until the custom font is ready, as discussed in Chapter 5, can improve LCP. However, using a *preload* tag for the font file can help as well because the *preload* tag instructs the browser to load the font file more quickly.

Use Faster Image Formats: WebP and AVIF

Choosing a faster image format can reduce LCP when the LCP element is an image. Most websites use PNG or JPEG image formats, with 82.1% of websites using PNGs and 77.9% of websites using JPEGs.[3] While these formats have historically been an appropriate choice for images, images saved in these formats have larger file sizes and load slower, often contributing to higher LCP. In contrast, images saved in the newer AVIF or WebP formats have smaller file sizes and load more efficiently.

Released by Google in 2010, WebP achieves smaller sizes by encoding images more efficiently. This format uses predictive algorithms to detect visually similar areas when transforming and caching image data. How much smaller WebP files are compared to JPEG, PNG, or GIF varies. Some reports show up to a 25–35% reduction in images of the same quality.

AVIF files were developed by AOMedia in 2019 to have even better compression algorithms than WebP images. Reports on savings using AVIF vary, with some reporting up to a 20% file size reduction compared to WebP.

The savings will be unique to each image, so different formats should be evaluated for each image. A tool like squoosh.app can be used to evaluate file size savings by using different image formats. Choosing the smallest size possible is important, especially when an image is the LCP element.

However, file size savings need to be balanced against image quality. Poor image quality worsens the user experience, so LCP should not be improved at the expense of user experience. The squoosh.app tool will also compare image quality across different formats. Typically, AVIF and WebP achieve an equivalent quality at a smaller file size given how the

---

[3] "Usage Statistics of Image File Formats for Websites." 2023. W3Techs. Q-Success. November 13, 2023. `https://w3techs.com/technologies/overview/image_format`

protocols have been developed. For certain images, PNG or JPEG formats may produce a higher quality image but the image quality gains are rarely significant enough to justify the increased file size.

WebP and AVIF files also offer many of the same features widely supported with PNG, JPEG, and GIF formats. AVIF and WebP files can be transparent, like PNG or GIF files. Both can be animated, like GIFs. However, when adding animation, a short video may load more efficiently than a GIF, AVIF, or WebP file. It is important to test different formats to determine whether an animated image or small video file loads more quickly with a faster LCP, and at an acceptable level of quality.

In addition, there is growing browser support for WebP and AVIF. Chrome has supported WebP since 2014, Edge since 2018, Firefox since 2019, and Safari since 2022.[4] AVIF is fully supported by Chrome as of 2020, Firefox as of 2021, and Safari as of 2023, but AVIF is not supported in Edge as of 2023.[5] To account for varied browser support, multiple formats can be created for an image and the browser can choose which format to use, based on what is supported. This can be done using the <picture> tag, as shown in the following code example. This code includes an AVIF, WebP, and JPEG file, with the AVIF file as the primary choice. The browser selects the first file type it can support for that image and once selected, the browser will only load and paint that one image file.

```
<picture>
  <source srcset="example-image.avif" type="image/avif">
  <source srcset="example-image.webp" type="image/webp">
  <img src="example-image.jpeg" alt="image description">
</picture>
```

---

[4] "WebP." Can I Use. Accessed November 13, 2023. https://caniuse.com/webp

[5] "AVIF Image Format." Can I Use. Accessed November 13, 2023. https://caniuse.com/avif

Recap: When to Use Largest Contentful Paint

LCP should be regularly monitored to identify when the largest piece of content is ready for visitors to see. As a part of Core Web Vitals, it should also be monitored to determine if slow LCP is impacting SEO performance.

- **Is the reporting scope meaningful?** LCP answers a specific and important question: when can visitors see the largest piece of content in the viewport? If LCP is slow, that means visitors are waiting longer to see important content. Along with regularly monitoring LCP to identify problems, LCP should also be tested on new website designs to see how painting times have changed.

- **Is it an effective business goal?** As a part of Core Web Vitals, LCP can influence where a page ranks in organic search results, especially in competitive search results. This makes it an important metric to include with regular monitoring. Along with the SEO impacts, LCP can also impact other business goals, including website conversions. One study from Web. dev found that conversion rates dropped 1.3% for each 100 milliseconds increase in LCP.[6] Some websites may see a higher or lower drop depending on that website's unique situation. Regardless of the exact percentage, a slower LCP means visitors waited longer for the main content to appear on the page, which will deter some visitors from engaging with the website or converting.

---

[6] Garcia, Manuel, Dikla Cohen, Patrícia Couto Neto, and Rui Santos. 2022. "Luxury Retailer Farfetch Sees Higher Conversion Rates for Better Core Web Vitals." Web. dev. July 12, 2022. https://web.dev/case-studies/farfetch

- **Does it describe the user experience?** If the largest part of the main content takes longer to load, that will create a poorer experience for visitors. LCP's definition of content is narrow and often the LCP element will be a key part of what people want to see on the page. Regularly monitoring LCP across the website will identify which pages have a poorer user experience. It can also be helpful to compare LCP to FCP. Comparing the two indicates how long it takes from when painting starts to when the largest piece of content is painted. A greater delay between FCP and LCP typically means visitors are waiting longer for main content to be painted.

- **How easy is it to improve?** Saving images to a different format or resizing a few images is typically an easy way to improve LCP. However, resaving or resizing images is more challenging at scale. Similarly, using *preload* or adjusting *fetchpriority* is relatively simple to do on a single page, but these tasks become more complicated across hundreds of pages. While sometimes a complicated change at scale, these types of changes are often worth the investment because they help files associated with the LCP element to load sooner. However, these types of changes should be tested carefully before being implemented. Adjusting priority to load some files sooner means loading other files later and loading other files later could worsen other speed metrics.

- **How impactful are improvements?** Improving LCP typically makes a noticeable impact on site speed. Visitors will notice if the largest item in the viewport takes too long to appear. By loading the largest item faster, the website will not only be faster for visitors, but will also feel faster for visitors. Improving LCP can also improve other paint metrics. While the browser is busy painting the webpage's LCP element, the browser is blocked from painting all other elements. If the browser can paint the largest element faster, then all other elements will also paint faster.

CHAPTER 9

Cumulative Layout Shift

Browsers do not wait to receive all webpage files before beginning to render the page. Instead, browsers will begin rendering once some elements are ready. For example, the webpage's main text may load quickly and will render first, but the header files, such as the logo or navigation CSS, may load slowly and will render later. As the browser loads additional files, executes additional code, and displays new elements, previously rendered elements may need to move from their initial position to a new position to make room for those new elements. Elements moving from one position to another can make it harder for visitors to use the page.

What Cumulative Layout Shift Measures

Cumulative Layout Shift (CLS) is a Core Web Vitals metric that measures how visually stable elements are on a webpage. Layout shifts are totaled within a session window where shifting occurs, and the session window with the largest total shifts is used as a page's CLS score.

© Matthew Edgar 2024
M. Edgar, *Speed Metrics Guide*, https://doi.org/10.1007/979-8-8688-0155-6_9

Shifting Elements

Every DOM element has a position on the page, represented by (X, Y) coordinates like those on a graph. This position is calculated during the layout stage of the rendering process. A shifting element is any element within the DOM that changes its position, vertically or horizontally, relative to the beginning of the document. For example, a paragraph may start at the coordinates of (82, 374) but then JavaScript code may cause that paragraph to move, or shift, to the coordinates (82, 604). In this example, there was no horizontal movement on the X axis, staying at 82, but there was movement on the Y axis, shifting vertically from position 374 to 604.

Layout Shift

The Layout Shift API that calculates shift scores evaluates the (X, Y) coordinates for all elements within each rendered frame. A rendered frame is a snapshot of the webpage at a specific time interval. When the layout is recalculated, a new frame is rendered, and the starting position of elements is evaluated. If the starting position changed between frames, a layout shift occurred.

Layout Shifts That Are Not Evaluated

There are three types of movements that are not considered shifts: changes in position due to a visitor scrolling down the page, changes made to the element's *transform* property, and changes made to the element's size. These actions do not change the rendered position relative to the beginning of the document. If this seems confusing, think of a website as a graph, with an X and Y axis, and each element placed somewhere on that graph. Scrolling will change the viewable portion of this graph but does not change the graph itself. Similarly, a change to an element's *transform* property may cause that element to rotate or scale, but it rotates or scales in the same place on the graph.

The way resizing impacts shifting is more nuanced. Consider an example where JavaScript code adds an image to an existing <div> tag. By adding that image, the <div>'s size will expand to fit the image. However, the <div> tag remains at the same starting position – the same coordinates on the graph – after that image is added. The <div> has not shifted. The image was added at a specific position and that position never changed, so the image has not shifted either. When that <div> resizes, though, other elements on the page below the <div> may need to shift to a different position to accommodate the <div>'s new size. If those other elements shift because of the <div>'s new size, then those other elements are the shifting elements.

Expected vs. Unexpected Shifts

Layout shifts are only a problem for visitors when they are unexpected. Unexpected layout shifts disrupt the experience, such as a video moving 100 pixels down the page while a visitor was watching it or a button shifting position just as a visitor was about to tap it. However, some layout shifts occur in response to a visitor's interaction. For example, clicking a "read more" button may cause elements to shift as the browser loads and paints additional text. Visitors would expect to see a layout shift when clicking this button, so that shift would not be disruptive.

Expected shifts must occur within 500 milliseconds of the interaction. When there is a recent interaction on an element from the visitor, the browser sets the *hadRecentInput* attribute to true to indicate that an interaction has occurred. The final CLS score only factors in layout shifts with the *hadRecentInput* attribute set to false.

How Layout Shifting Is Scored

Two variables are multiplied together to calculate the layout shift score.

- **Distance fraction:** ratio representing how far the element shifted within the viewport.

- **Impact fraction:** a ratio representing how much of the viewport was affected by the shift.

An example of distance fraction is shown in Figure 9-1. In this example, the page was initially rendered into the viewport, the part of the page visitors can see on their device, as pictured on the left, with a simple paragraph of text. An image was later loaded and painted above the paragraph, as pictured on the right. The addition of the image shifted the paragraph down the page, though kept the paragraph within the viewport. The distance the paragraph shifted is represented by the arrow. The distance fraction represents how far the element shifted relative to the size of the viewport. In this example, that arrow is about one-third of the viewport's height. That would make the distance fraction approximately 0.33 in this example.

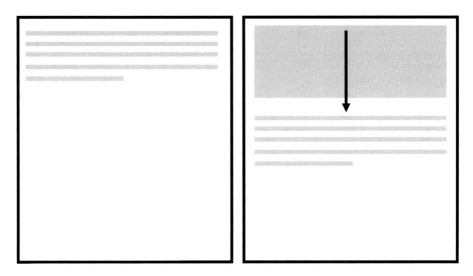

Figure 9-1. *Distance fraction – the amount the paragraph shifted is represented by the arrow*

Figure 9-2 shows an example of impact fraction in the same example scenario where a paragraph shifted after an image was loaded and painted. The impact fraction measures how much of the viewport was affected by the shift. In this example, the paragraph shifted from the top third of the viewport to the middle third of the viewport. The dashed rectangle highlights the impacted area, which is about two-thirds of the viewport in this example. That would make the impact fraction 0.67. Multiplying the impact fraction by the distance fraction, 0.67 x 0.33, this shift has a score of 0.22.

Figure 9-2. *Impact fraction – the area impacted by the shift is indicated by the dashed-line box*

While speed tools will perform these calculations, understanding how a layout shift score is calculated makes it easier to interpret that score. A larger layout shift score means that elements either shifted a greater distance on the page or affected a larger area of the page during the shift. If the shift cannot be avoided entirely, the solution is to minimize how far the element shifted or minimize the area impacted by the shift. Shifting across a smaller distance or within a smaller area of the viewport reduces how problematic the shift is for visitors.

Session Windows

CLS is no longer a total of all layout shifts that occur across a person's visit to the webpage. Instead, layout shifts are measured within session windows. A session window starts when the first layout shift is detected. The browser will keep the session window open and wait for another shift to occur for one second. Any shifts that occur within that second will be part of the same window. The window will close if no additional layout shifts are detected one second after the last detected shift. If multiple layout shifts are detected, then the session window will close after a total duration of five seconds. A new window is started if additional shifts are detected after the first window closes.

In the example shown in Figure 9-3, a layout shift was detected, so a new session window was started. Before one second passed, another layout shift was detected so the session window remained open for an additional second to detect any additional shifts that occurred. In this example, the shift score is represented on the vertical axis and the elapsed time is represented on the horizontal axis.

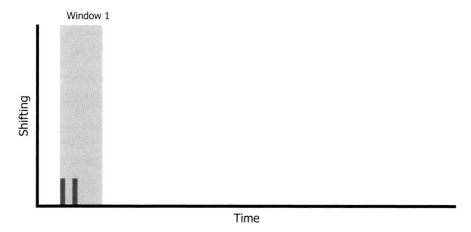

Figure 9-3. *The start of a new session window with two shifts detected so far*

Each shift is scored as it is detected and then the scores are totaled for all shifts occurring within that window. Figure 9-4 shows a longer session window. There are six total shifts within this window and each shift has a score of 0.02. These shifts add up to a total shift score of .12 for this session window.

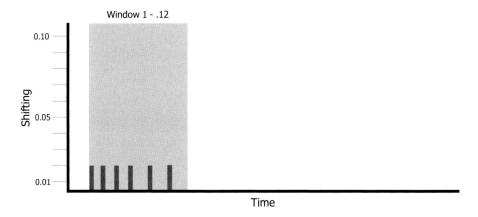

Figure 9-4. *Scoring Window 1 with six layout shifts*

There can be multiple session windows during a person's visit to the page. The window with the maximum score will be used for the webpage's final CLS measurement. Figure 9-5 shows three windows. The first window has a total score of .12. The second window has one shift, adding up to a total score of .10. The third window has a total score of .08. In this example, CLS would be measured using the first window's total score because this window has the largest layout shift score across all session windows.

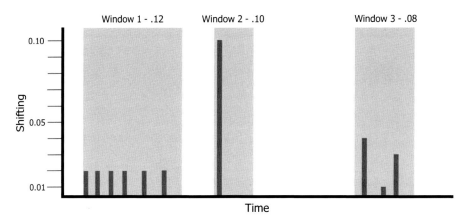

Figure 9-5. *Three session windows showing the cumulative shifting scores for each window*

All layout shifts are a problem, even if those shifts occur outside the session window with the most shifting. In this example, the larger shift in Window 2 may represent a bigger problem for visitors than the smaller layout shifts in Window 1. Alternatively, the elements that shifted in Windows 1 or 2 may not be as noticeable for visitors compared to the elements that shifted in Window 3.

How CLS Relates to Speed

Slower speeds are a common cause of layout shifting, which is why Google includes CLS as a Core Web Vitals metric. For example, late-running JavaScript code often causes shifting. The browser loads and executes late-running JavaScript code after the page's layout was initially calculated. When late-running JavaScript code is eventually executed by the browser, it can add new DOM elements. The browser must recalculate and update the layout to account for those new DOM elements. Those updates can cause other elements to shift unexpectedly. Late-running JavaScript code can also change the position of existing elements, causing those elements to shift.

Shifting can also happen because of late-loading images or videos. When images arrive later, the browser inserts the image where it belongs. Unless space is reserved for the image, the image's size will only be determined after it loads. This forces the browser to update the layout and that causes other elements below the late-loading image to shift around the page. Using the lazy loading attribute, discussed in Chapter 5, will avoid this issue because it paints the image before it appears in the viewport. Shifts that occur outside the viewport are not seen by visitors and are not factored into CLS.

Measuring Cumulative Layout Shift

Layout shifting should be evaluated on each page of the website as each page may have unique elements that contribute to shifting. Also, shifting should be tested on different device types because there will be unique layouts for mobile and desktop devices. Testing across different connection speeds may expose additional shifting because slower connection speeds can delay JavaScript or image files, resulting in more late-loading files.

CLS Benchmarks

Per Google's Core Web Vitals guidelines, the final CLS score for a page should be 0.1 or less to be in an acceptable range and a score of 0.25 or greater is considered poor.[1] According to data from HTTP Archive, 68.3% of desktop websites and 76% of mobile websites have a CLS score under 0.1.[2]

Identify What Shifts and Session Windows: WebPageTest

The first question to answer is what elements are shifting and by how much? One way to identify shifting elements is with the Web Vitals report in WebPageTest (`www.webpagetest.org/`). After running a test, select "Web Vitals" from the "View" menu and scroll to the "Cumulative Layout Shift" section of this report. Figure 9-6 shows an example of this report with three session windows. The first session window in this report, Window 3, has the greatest amount of shifting with a score of 0.2. Windows 1 and 2 have a score of 0, with only a minimal amount of shifting. The shifting element is highlighted and hovering over the image will show where that element was positioned before it shifted (the hovering is not pictured).

---

[1] McQuade, Bryan. 2022. "Defining the Core Web Vitals Metrics Thresholds." Web.dev. July 18, 2022. `https://web.dev/articles/ defining-core-web-vitals-thresholds`

[2] "Report: CrUX." 2023. HTTP Archive. October 1, 2023. `https://httparchive. org/reports/chrome-ux-report#cruxSmallCls`

Cumulative Layout Shift (0.2)

View as Filmstrip - View Video - About Cumulative Layout Shift (CLS)

Window 3 (0.2)

Hover over any image to see the previous frame and the effect of the layout shift.

29104... (0.19959)

Window 1 (0)

Hover over any image to see the previous frame and the effect of the layout shift.

1775... (0.00025)

Window 2 (0)

Hover over any image to see the previous frame and the effect of the layout shift.

8676... (0.00009)

Figure 9-6. *WebPageTest – Web Vitals Report – showing shifts in different session windows*

WebPageTest also offers a filmstrip and a video recording to better understand what is shifting and when the shifting happens. Click the "View as Filmstrip" or "View Video" links on the "Cumulative Layout Shift" report to access these features. An example of the filmstrip is shown in Figure 9-7. In this example, a large hero image was present on the page at the 29 second mark but at the 29.5 second mark, that hero image shifted down the page. The hero image consumed a large amount of the viewport, and it shifted almost completely outside the viewport, resulting in a large impact area and a large shift distance.

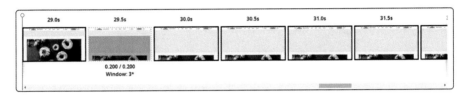

Figure 9-7. *WebPageTest – Filmstrip view showing a layout shift*

The example shown in Figures 9-6 and 9-7 only showed a single element shifting during a session window. However, there can be multiple shifts within the same session window and those can also be seen in WebPageTest's reports. The example in Figure 9-8 shows a session window where multiple elements shifted. To view these shifts on the "Filmstrip View" report, it can be helpful to click the "Adjust Filmstrip Settings" button and change the "Thumbnail Interval" to a lower value, like 0.1 second instead of the default 0.5 second. Figure 9-9 indicates this button with an arrow and provides an example of how this adjusts the filmstrip report. This adjustment clarifies what is shifting within the first session window and when the shifting happens.

Cumulative Layout Shift (0.266)

View as Filmstrip - View Video - About Cumulative Layout Shift (CLS) ⌐

Window 1 (0.266)

Hover over any image to see the previous frame and the effect of the layout shift.

2116 — (0.18719)

1999 — (0.04840)

2051 — (0.02888)

2154 — (0.00059)

Figure 9-8. *Multiple shifts in the same window, as shown in WebPageTest's Web Vitals report*

Figure 9-9. *WebPageTest filmstrip view adjusted to a 0.1 second interval*

Find Shifting Element Coordinates and Viewport Size: Chrome DevTools

Chrome DevTools also provides reports to understand shifting elements. In Google Chrome, before opening a webpage, right click and choose "Inspect." Once the Chrome DevTools area opens, click "Performance" in the top bar. This link may be hidden behind the ">>" icon. Once the "Performance" panel opens, click the record button and then load the page to test.

In the "Performance" panel, look for the section labeled "Layout Shifts" and search for any layout shifts that have been recorded. This may require zooming to specific sections of the timeline. Once a shift is identified, click it and the panel below will show a summary of the shift. An example of the "Layout Shifts" section with the "Summary" panel is shown in Figure 9-10.

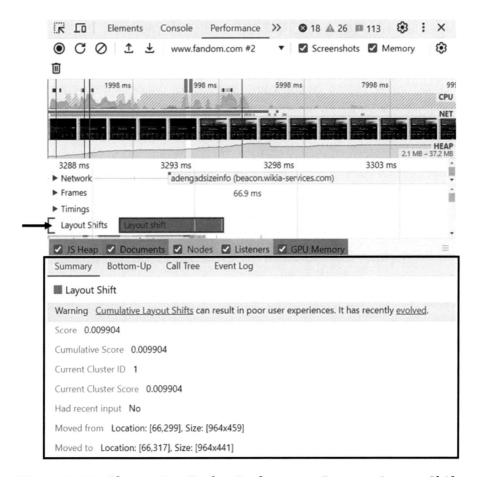

Figure 9-10. *Chrome DevTools – Performance Report – Layout Shifts with Summary*

The "Summary" panel provides the score for this layout shift, .009904 in this example, and indicates whether this shift was a result of user input. This data also provides the "Moved from" and "Moved to" coordinates, indicating the position and size of the elements in the viewport before and after it shifted.

The "Moved from" and "Moved to" coordinates give a sense of the shift's impact and the distance the element shifted. In the example shown in Figure 9-10, the element moved from position (66, 299) to position (66, 317). This means it shifted vertically 18 pixels but did not shift horizontally. The element's width remained the same at 964 pixels, but the height changed from 459 pixels to 441 pixels. The height reduced because a portion of the element shifted off the screen and was no longer in the viewport. Only shifting in the viewport is factored into a layout shift score. Still, this is a wide and tall element and consumes more of the screen, so the shift will have a greater impact area even if the distance shifted is relatively small.

Hovering over the "Moved from" row will highlight the element's starting position before it shifted, and the "Moved to" row will highlight the position of the element after it shifted. The example shown in Figure 9-11 shows a shift with the "In the News" section of this webpage. The top image in Figure 9-11 highlights the moved from area, where "In the News" section was located before it shifted. The area highlighted overlaps other content on the page, indicating loading that other content may have caused the section being evaluated to move lower. The bottom image in Figure 9-11 highlights the area where the "In the News" section shifted to lower in the viewport.

Figure 9-11. *Chrome DevTools – Performance Report – moved from and moved to positions are in the highlighted region*

Ways to Improve Cumulative Layout Shift

Unexpected shifting means the browser did not have all the necessary information when initially calculating the page's layout. The browser was forced to update the layout and shift elements around the page when new information was provided. Unexpected shifting can be avoided by ensuring the browser has all necessary information as early as possible. That can be done by loading files that are important for the page's layout more quickly or by instructing the browser to reserve space for elements that will load later.

Identify Late-Running JavaScript Files

Ad scripts are one of the most common late-running JavaScript files and are a common reason shifting occurs. In Figure 9-12, the left image shows the page on an initial load with an empty space reserved for the ad. The right image shows the page once an ad has loaded (the ad is intentionally hidden from view). The ad loads at a larger size than the empty space, causing that section of the page to expand to fit the ad. Expanding that section causes the other webpage content to shift lower.

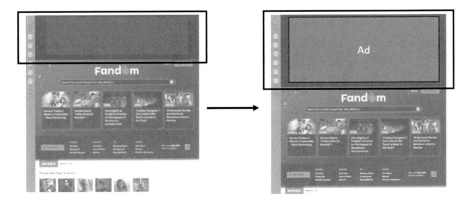

Figure 9-12. *An ad loading causes a layout shift, shifting screenshots from Chrome DevTools*

This shifting happens because the ad scripts load later, and the browser does not have the information about the ad when the page is initially painted. One option to fix shifting is to load the ad scripts earlier. That way, the browser loads and paints the ad sooner, accounting for the ad's final size, before painting other elements. For example, in Figure 9-12, if the ad was painted before the other page content, then the browser would initially paint the section containing the ad at the final size and no shifting would occur. Using *preload* or *fetchpriority,* discussed in Chapter 4, will give ad scripts a higher priority and instruct the browser to load those ad scripts more quickly.

Loading the ad script earlier requires identifying these late-running files that cause shifting and determining when that ad is loaded. This can be done in Chrome DevTools. Open Chrome DevTools and click the "Network" link in the top menu. Finding this link may require clicking the ">>" icon. Once "Network" is open, refresh the page. Then, use the search box to filter for the ad script. Typically, this can be found by the ad script's domain name or by searching for the word "ad". Filtering to "JS" first and scrolling through file names may be another way to identify what file is loading the ad. An example is shown in Figure 9-13 and filters using the word "adview," which is the name of the file that loads ads on this page.

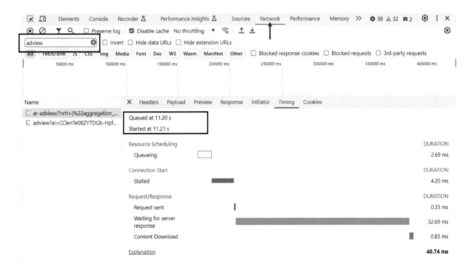

Figure 9-13. *Use Chrome DevTools Network report to identify late-running scripts*

After finding the file, click the file name to show an additional panel with more details. Click the "Timing" link to see when this file was queued and started loading. In the example shown in Figure 9-13, this ad script was queued for loading at 11.20 seconds and started loading at 11.21 seconds. It then took 40.74 seconds for this script to load. That much of a delay could result in shifting when the ad eventually loads.

This same method can be used to identify other late-loading files that cause shifting, including images or videos. However, not all late-loading files will cause shifting. An image, ad, or video loading late, will only cause shifting if loading that file requires the browser to update the page layout and shift other elements to make room for the late-loading file. This leads to the second way of fixing layout shifting: reserving space.

Reserve Space

Loading ad scripts, images, or videos earlier may delay other important files. For example, loading an ad sooner may delay loading a font file or an important image. Delaying a font file or an image can delay painting, worsening Largest Contentful Paint and other paint-related metrics. The delay could also make the page more difficult for visitors to use. An ad is rarely the most critical piece of content to load relative to other content. The same could be said for videos and decorative images. Increasing the priority of an ad may be the only way to fix shifting, but ideally only the most important files should be given a higher priority.

The better answer instead of adjusting priority is to reserve space on the page. For example, when the width and height are not provided for an image, the browser will not reserve space for the image prior to its loading. Once the image loads, the browser will calculate the width and height of the image and update the page layout accordingly. Those layout updates can cause other elements to shift, as shown in Figures 9-1 and 9-2 earlier in the chapter.

The solution is to add *width* and *height* attributes to the image. The following code specifies a *width* and *height* of 200 pixels each. This could also be defined in the CSS and media queries could be used to set the width and height of the image on different screen sizes.

```
<img src="example-image.png" width="200" height="200">
```

If these attributes were specified in Figures 9-1 and 9-2, then no shifting would occur. Instead, the browser would reserve a space of 200 pixels x 200 pixels for this example image, as shown by the dashed line on the right side of Figure 9-14. When the image is then loaded and painted, the browser replaces the empty area on the page. The layout for the paragraph of text below the image does not need to be recalculated. Note that *height* is the more important attribute to specify in this example since the shifting happens vertically, not horizontally.

Figure 9-14. *With space reserved for the image, no shifting occurs when the image is loaded and painted*

With variable sized elements, like ads, a specific width and height cannot be provided. The ad may load at 200 pixels tall in some instances and load at 300 pixels tall in others. Instead, a minimum height or minimum width can be provided. This will not prevent shifting but will minimize the amount of shifting that occurs. The minimum height or width specifies the starting height or width of an area on the page. The area will be resized when an ad or other content loads to this area of the page, but the difference between the starting size and the final size will not be as great. That lessens the impact and distance of the shifting.

This can be done with *min-width* and *min-height* properties in the CSS code. For example, the following example code specifies a minimum height of 200 pixels for a <div> with the class ad-area. The browser will reserve 200 pixels of space for this <div> when the website layout is initially calculated. If the ad later loads at 250 pixels tall, the <div> will resize accordingly to accommodate. This increased size may cause other elements to shift; however, only 50 pixels of shifting would occur. Had no *min-height* been defined, then 250 pixels of shifting would have occurred when the ad was loaded instead. Media queries can be used to adjust the *min-height* and *min-width* for different screen sizes.

```
div.ad-area {
  min-height: 200px;
}
```

To visualize *min-height*, refer to Figure 9-12. That website provided a *min-height* for the ad section at the top of the page. While shifting still happened when the ad loaded, the amount of shifting was minimized thanks to the *min-height* reserving some amount of space. Potentially, an opportunity for that website would be to reserve a greater amount of height if the ad commonly loads at a larger size.

Recap: When to Use Cumulative Layout Shift

CLS should be regularly monitored to identify how much shifting is happening across the website and to identify which pages have the most shifting. CLS is also a part of Core Web Vitals, so regular monitoring will detect if poor CLS scores impact SEO performance.

- **Is the reporting scope meaningful?** Shifting is evaluated across the entire visit to the webpage, with shifting broken into session windows. That gives CLS a wider view over the visit to the page compared to other metrics that are focused on specific aspects of the page load. The session window can make CLS harder to understand, as can calculating impact and distance fractions. However, the basic idea within CLS is meaningful: a higher score means more shifting occurred on the page and made the page harder for visitors to use.

- **Is it an effective business goal?** As part of Google's Core Web Vitals, CLS is an important metric to regularly monitor and poor CLS scores may negatively affect SEO performance. CLS may not always be an effective speed KPI. While more shifting can impact conversions and engagements, the impact is dependent on which elements are shifting. A shifting "Add to Cart" button will have a bigger impact on business goals than a shifting decorative image. To be most effective, CLS needs to be qualified with an explanation of what is shifting. That qualification is easier to include within regular monitoring instead of in reports to stakeholders.

- **Does it describe the user experience?** CLS describes a problem that can create a poor experience for visitors. The more things shift on the page, the more frustrating the page will be for visitors. If CLS is caused because of slower loading files, there will be other problems making the webpage even more difficult to use.

- **How easy is it to improve?** Layout shifting is not always easy to improve. Reserving appropriate space for all elements is not always possible, especially with highly dynamic content. Loading JavaScript, images, and other files more efficiently can reduce shifting. Also, many of the files that cause shifting are third-party scripts, especially ads, so there is only so much a company can do to improve how efficiently those third-party scripts load.

- **How impactful are improvements?** CLS improvements have a big impact on conversion rates and the user experience more broadly but do not always have an impact on other speed metrics. If layout shifting happens because space was not properly reserved, defining dimensions to reserve space will not improve the website's loading process. If layout shifting is caused by late-running JavaScript files, improving CLS may also improve other speed metrics, including Total Blocking Time. However, it is just as possible that improving CLS may slow other metrics. Changing a late-running JavaScript file to load earlier might delay loading and painting other files. That could worsen other metrics, like First Contentful Paint or Largest Contentful Paint. To make CLS improvements as beneficial as possible, it is important to evaluate any trade-offs between CLS and other metrics.

CHAPTER 10

Interaction to Next Paint

After enough of the webpage has been loaded and painted, visitors can begin interacting with the page. These interactions change something about the webpage, such as displaying a new image or playing a video. The browser must do additional work to process these changes. Some of the work can be quite extensive and take considerable time to complete. For some types of changes, the browser also needs to request additional files from the server and the server will require additional time to process those requested files. The more work the browser or the server must do in response to visitor interactions, the longer it will take for visitors to see changes in response to their interactions. This creates a poorer experience for visitors and may deter visitors from interacting further.

What Interaction to Next Paint Measures

Interaction to Next Paint (INP) is a Core Web Vitals metric that measures how long it takes the website to show a visual response to a visitor's interaction.

Events and Event Handler Code

Visitor interactions trigger events in the browser. For example, when a visitor taps on a button, it triggers the *click* event or when a visitor presses a key on the keyboard (virtual or physical), a *keydown* event is triggered. Event handler code is written in JavaScript and listens for specific events to be triggered. Some event handler code might listen for any *click* event or other code might listen for a *click* event only on a specific button. When the event specified in that event handler code is triggered, the browser executes the related event handler code. Part of the event handler code can show a response to the visitor's interactions, which will update the display of the webpage.

As an example, consider a scenario where a visitor taps a button and additional text appears. When the visitor taps that button, the *click* event is triggered. The browser searches for any event handler code associated with *click* events for that button and executes any associated code found. Since this example event handler code loads additional text to the page, the JavaScript code will likely contain some type of request for the additional text from the server. The browser will send the request for that text as part of executing this code. The server receives and processes this request then sends the additional text to the browser. The browser parses the HTML for the new text it has received and recalculates the page layout to determine how to place the new text into the existing page. Once parsing and layout are complete, the browser paints the new text for the visitor to see. In this example, INP measures how long it takes between the visitor tapping the button and when the visitor sees the new text appearing on the screen.

Interaction Process

The browser's response to visitor's interactions includes three steps, also shown in Figure 10-1:

1. **Input Delay:** After an event is triggered, the browser waits for other tasks to finish running before it can execute the related event handler code. In Figure 10-1, the visitor's interaction is marked by the first vertical bar. When the visitor interacts, there is another task already running, so the browser must wait for that task to finish before it can respond to the interaction. If this sounds similar to Total Blocking Time discussed in Chapter 6, it should – more details are provided about how these metrics relate later in this chapter.

2. **Processing Time:** After it begins executing the event handler code, the browser needs time to process that code. In Figure 10-1, the event handler code is executed starting with the second vertical bar. This initiates a new task that runs on the main thread. During this task, the browser is executing the event handler code. Some code is more involved than others and will take longer to run, such as scripts that load additional resources to the page. Other code may run more quickly, but processing time is dependent on the speed of the visitor's device.

3. **Presentation Delay:** Finally, the browser updates the website with the result of the code. For example, if a visitor clicked a button to load a new video, the browser needs to update the page to show that video. In Figure 10-1, the third vertical bar marks

when the browser starts the paint operations related to the task. There can be a delay between the start of these operations and when a visitor sees the update. This delay happens because the browser needs to parse additional HTML code, recalculate the page layout to determine where to place new elements, and then, finally, paint those new elements to the page.

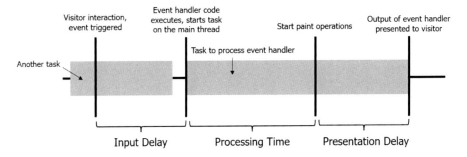

Figure 10-1. *Interaction process showing a single task on the main thread*

Measuring Interactions

INP does not evaluate all interactions. Only interaction times associated with clicks, taps, or key presses are measured. Key press interactions are measured on physical or virtual keyboards. Time associated with hovering or scrolling interactions will not contribute to INP.

All page interactions are assessed and the final INP for a visitor's session with that page will be the longest INP measured. However, knowing that there can be occasional disruptions even on the best webpages, INP measurements will ignore the highest interaction for every 50 interactions. Most pages will not have that many interactions.

How INP Relates to FID

First Input Delay (FID) was a Core Web Vitals metric until March 2024 when it was replaced by INP. Both FID and INP are ways of measuring interaction times. However, there are two main differences between FID and INP.

First, FID only measures the Input Delay step of the interaction process, ignoring the Processing Time and Presentation Time of the interaction. In Figure 10-1, Input Delay is the time between the first and second vertical bars. This narrower scope makes FID less useful than INP because the full interaction process is not measured.

Second, FID only measures Input Delay for the visitor's first interaction with the webpage. The first interaction may be faster than other interactions. So, FID may be within an acceptable range even though there are other interaction-related problems present. In contrast, INP evaluates the interaction process across all interactions and, therefore, provides a better understanding of how visitors experience interacting with the entirety of the webpage.

To understand the difference, consider an example where a visitor clicks three buttons on a page and triggers the *click* event three times. FID only measures the Input Delay for the first of those three button clicks. INP measures the time for the full interaction process– Input Delay, Processing Time, and Presentation Time – for each button click. After the three interaction times are measured, the page's final INP will be the button click with the longest interaction time.

How INP Relates to the DOM

To change the visual display of the page, the event handler code needs to update the webpage's Document Object Model (DOM). The DOM, as discussed in Chapter 3, represents all the HTML elements on the page. The event handler code needs to step through the DOM to figure out which elements need to be updated or may need to be added to the DOM. For example, event handler code might update text in an existing <p> tag or might add a new <img> tag to the page. The larger the DOM, the longer it will take to make these changes. As a result, a larger DOM size will require the browser to do more work when executing event handler code, slowing INP.

How INP Compares to Total Blocking Time and Time to Interactive

Input Delay is a result of blocking tasks. If the main thread is busy processing other tasks, the browser will be unable to respond quickly to visitor interactions. The longer the blocking time across all tasks, as measured by Total Blocking Time (TBT), the longer the browser will delay a response. When there is a higher TBT, Input Delay will often be higher as well and that will cause INP to be slower. If Input Delay is the reason for higher INP, then the primary solution is reducing TBT.

INP and Time to Interactive (TTI) both describe aspects of how quickly visitors can interact with the webpage and indicate if there are any disruptions that will delay those interactions. The difference is that TTI reflects a potential disruption for visitors and INP reflects an actual disruption for visitors. This difference results from how TTI and INP are measured. As discussed in Chapter 6, speed test tools calculate TTI by finding a quiet window on the main thread and looking back to see when the last long task occurred before that quiet window. TTI can only be measured in synthesized tests run by speed test tools. When TTI is slow, visitors may experience slower interaction times. In contrast, INP is measured for real-world visitors. When INP is slow, it means visitors did experience slower interaction times. This makes a slow INP a higher priority than a slow TTI.

Measuring Interaction to Next Paint

Interaction times should be measured for each interactive element on a webpage. Some webpages will have more interactive elements than others. Templated pages may have similar interactive elements, so testing interaction times on a few pages built using the same template may be sufficient to identify issues. How visitors can interact with a webpage will differ between mobile and desktop devices, so interaction times should be measured on different device types.

INP Benchmarks

According to Google's Core Web Vitals guidelines, INP should be less than 200 milliseconds and an INP greater than 500 milliseconds will be considered slow.[1] According to HTTP Archive's data assessing millions of websites, 96.8% of desktop websites meet this threshold, but only 64.9% of mobile websites have an INP under 200 milliseconds.[2]

Simulate Interactions: DebugBear's INP Profiler

INP measures real delays visitors experience when interacting with the website. The best way to measure this is by reviewing real world data in the Chrome User Experience Report (CrUX) dataset, using a tool like PageSpeed Insights, discussed in Appendix B. There will be no CrUX data, however, for pages that do not have real-world visitors, including newly

---

[1] Wagner, Jeremy. 2023. "Interaction to Next Paint (INP)." Web.dev. June 28, 2023. `https://web.dev/articles/inp`

[2] "Report: CrUX." 2023. HTTP Archive. October 1, 2023. `https://httparchive.org/reports/chrome-ux-report#cruxFastInp`

published pages or pages currently in development. For these types of pages, interactions can be simulated using DebugBear's INP Profiler (`www.debugbear.com/inp-debugger`).

This tool loads a page on either mobile or desktop devices, interacts automatically with page elements, and reports on the interaction duration for each of those elements. The example report in Figure 10-2 shows it took 704 milliseconds for the webpage to respond to a typing interaction in the main search bar and that it took 578 milliseconds for the webpage to respond after clicking a button. This is a simulation, so real-world interaction times may differ, but this tool highlights which interactions might present a bigger problem for real-world visitors.

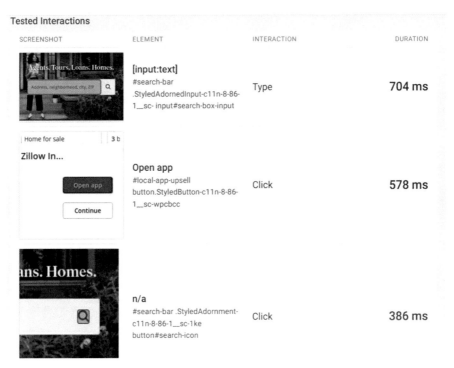

Figure 10-2. *DebugBear INP Profiler example result*

Breakdown INP: Web Vitals Extension

After identifying which elements may have slower interaction times, the next question is: what part of the interaction process causes slower speeds? The steps to take to improve INP will change depending on whether Input Delay, Processing Time, or Presentation Delay is the reason for slower speeds.

The Google Chrome Web Vitals extension (`https://bit.ly/3tkpL5k`) provides details about each part of the interaction process. Once added to Google Chrome, this extension will present information about all the Core Web Vitals metrics in the browser's Console. To view the browser's Console in Google Chrome, right click on any page of the website and then select "Inspect". Click "Console" in the upper navigation bar. With Console open, start interacting with the page and data about INP from this extension will begin to appear.

Figure 10-3 shows the Web Vitals extension data for an interaction with a button on the webpage. This button has an INP of 1064 milliseconds. Clicking the summary row will show more details, as seen in Figure 10-3. These details include the interaction target, which, in this case, is a button with the text "Load More" and a table detailing each part of the interaction process. For this button, Input Delay is only 1 millisecond and Presentation Delay is only 20 milliseconds, so neither are a major concern. However, Processing Time is 1044 milliseconds, which is what makes this interaction slower.

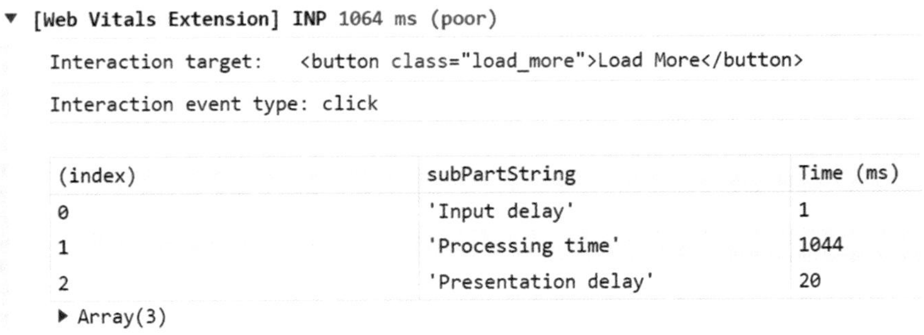

```
▼ [Web Vitals Extension] INP 1064 ms (poor)

    Interaction target:    <button class="load_more">Load More</button>

    Interaction event type: click
```

(index)	subPartString	Time (ms)
0	'Input delay'	1
1	'Processing time'	1044
2	'Presentation delay'	20

▶ Array(3)

Figure 10-3. *Web Vitals Extension showing INP data with a longer processing time*

Find Event Handler Code: Firefox DevTools

If INP problems are identified on a specific element, then the next step is to find and review the event handler code attached to that element. An easy way to find the code associated with an element is with Firefox's DevTools. After loading a webpage in Firefox, right click the problematic element, like a link or button, then click "Inspect". This will open Firefox DevTools's Inspector and show the code for the inspected element. If there is event handler code attached to this element, there will be a bubble containing the word "event" next to it. Clicking the "event" bubble will show the event handler code.

Figure 10-4 shows the Inspector for a link with the "event" bubble. This figure also shows the popup shown after clicking the bubble. That popup lists all the event handler code associated with this element and what event type each event handler uses. In this example, there are three event handlers, each using a *click* event. The second of these event handlers is expanded to show the event handler code. Once found, this code can be reviewed in more detail to identify improvement opportunities.

Figure 10-4. *Firefox DevTools – Inspector showing a link's event handler code*

Ways to Improve Interaction to Next Paint

An interaction time is made of three parts: Input Delay, Processing Time, Presentation Delay. Each part needs to be improved in different ways. If a slow Input Delay is worsening INP, the recommendations discussed in Chapter 6 to improve TBT will also help improve INP. If Processing Time is slower, then the focus should be on optimizing event handler code to understand what that code does and making that code run more efficiently. If Presentation Delay is slower, then reducing DOM size or simplifying CSS code, including optimizing animations, can improve INP.

Processing Time: Improve Event Handler Code

After finding the event handler code for elements with slow INP, it is important to understand what the code does and why that code is slowing INP. From there, opportunities can be found to optimize the JavaScript code. While knowing how to read and write JavaScript code can help in this process, assessing event handler code is not exclusively a task for developers. Non-developers can perform an initial review of the JavaScript code to answer some basic questions about what the code does to determine what code should be optimized.

- **How much code is there?** The more code that is present within a single event handler, the more impact this may have on INP. The problem, of course, is not strictly the volume of code but more about what that code is doing. Code that relies on an excessive number of loops or conditionals may run more slowly. Therefore, when reviewing the event handler code, check how many references to loops, indicated by the words *while* and *for*, and look for references to complex conditional statements, indicated by the words *if* or *else*. These are not necessarily problematic, but when INP is already high, each of these loops and conditionals is worth examining with a developer to see if each is necessary and how each contributes to INP.

- **Does the event handler load other files?** If the event handler code requires other files to load before painting a response, this can result in longer processing times. For example, clicking a button may load a new image or the code might fetch data from a remote file. This is harder to find within the code itself, but is easier to identify using Chrome DevTools Network report, discussed in Chapter 4. Open the Chrome DevTools Network report and then interact with the element with the high INP. If that element adds new files to the page, those files will be added to the Network report, increasing the number of requests. The Network report will also report the byte size of the element added. The more files that are added and the larger the size of those files, the more this may worsen Processing Time and, therefore, worsen INP.

- **How much does the event handler code update the DOM?** The new content added to a page by the event handler is wrapped in HTML code. The browser will need to parse that new HTML code and add it to the DOM. A few lines of HTML code will not present a problem, but an excessive amount of HTML would. Similarly, event handler code that updates multiple DOM elements will also take longer to process. If the DOM is already quite large, these DOM manipulations can have an even greater impact on INP. When reviewing the code, look for references to *createElement*, *innerHTML* or *appendChild* to find instances where the DOM is being updated. DOM size can also be measured before and after an interaction using the Performance Monitor in Chrome DevTools, discussed in Chapter 3.

- **Does the event handler prioritize sending a visual response to visitors?** The event handler code should prioritize painting over other operations. For example, it is common for event handler code to track interactions in a web analytics tool along with performing the main task. The code to track interactions should only run after all paint operations are completed. The references to *createElement*, *innerHTML*, or *appendChild* that update the DOM should be placed as high in the event handler code as possible. If those references are lower in the event handler code, it is worth questioning why and seeing if they can be called earlier.

For non-developers, generative AI tools can also help assess what the event handler code is doing and identify slower parts of the code that are worth fixing. An example response from ChatGPT in Figure 10-5 walks through event handler code for a given element, explaining what it does and what might be worth optimizing within the code. Along with pasting in the code, the prompt should also ask these tools to explain line-by-line what the code does as it relates to interactions and identify slower parts of the code.

Figure 10-5. *ChatGPT's response explaining what event handler code does and why the code may be slower*

Presentation Delay: Optimize Animations

To improve the user experience, some interactions update the display using animations. Sliding in additional text or images can be more appealing visually than having text or images suddenly appear on the page. However, animations can slow INP because it adds tasks for the browser to complete to render that animation.

How much impact the animation has depends on what tasks the animation must complete during the rendering process. There are three main steps to rendering an animation:

1. Updating styles and the render tree. The render tree is the DOM, representing the HTML on the page, and CSSOM, representing the CSS code. These were discussed in Chapters 3 and 5.

2. Calculating the layout, including updating the position and size of each element. To calculate the layout, the browser moves through the DOM to update the layout for each element affected by the animation.

3. Painting the animation and all associated elements to the screen. Some elements are added in separate layers on the page. Elements in separate layers and animations affecting those elements are painted separately – this is called compositing.

Not all animations need to go through all three steps. Some animations only affect painting or compositing while others update styles and layout as well. The more rendering steps the animation requires, the more the animation can delay INP. This is often discussed in terms of the animation cost, with some animations being more expensive. To improve INP, it is important to use cheaper animations.

- Expensive animations require all three steps. The most expensive step is recalculating the page layout. For example, an animation might change the width and height of a block of text. To perform this animation, the browser updates that block of text's styles with the new dimensions and then calculates the updated layout for that block. Once recalculated, the browser repaints the block of text. However, changing the width and height may also affect other elements. As discussed in Chapter 3, the DOM operates as a hierarchy. When an element changes, elements directly above or below that element in the DOM hierarchy may need to change as well. This can result in a ripple effect throughout the webpage's DOM, which adds to the animation cost. The animation cost grows if the DOM size is larger.

- Less expensive animations skip the step of the browser calculating a new layout. The animations still require updating styles and repainting to the page. For example, an animation may change the color of an element, such as adding a background color to highlight a part of the page. When the animation begins, the browser updates the affected element's styles with the new color and paints the new color. However, no positions or sizes change, so the page's layout is not updated, saving time.

- The cheapest animations are those that do not calculate a new layout and do not require repainting. These animations still update styles but do so in a compositor thread. The compositor thread is separate from the browser's main thread. This separation prevents the style calculation from blocking other tasks that need to run on the main thread. There are only two cheap animations: *transform* and *opacity*. With *transform*, elements can be rotated, scaled, and skewed. The *opacity* animation changes the element's transparency, which can be used to fade elements in or out of view in response to an interaction. Using these cheaper animation styles where possible is the most effective way to reduce INP, while still using animations to update the page.

Recap: When to Use Interaction to Next Paint

Regularly monitoring INP is helpful to understand how quickly visitors can interact with the page. Because INP is a part of Core Web Vitals, it should also be monitored to detect any impacts on SEO performance.

- **Is the reporting scope meaningful?** INP is a useful metric to understand how long it takes a visitor to interact with elements on a particular webpage. Poor interaction times are often related to other load problems, like a busier main thread or poorly optimized JavaScript code. INP has a broader scope than FID, evaluating the entire interaction process for all interactions with the page. That scope makes this metric more meaningful and a useful way to identify if problems exist in how visitors interact with a page.

- **Is it an effective business goal?** Faster interaction times will typically correspond with better conversion and engagement rates, making a clearer connection between INP and business goals. This can make INP

197

an effective metric to use as a speed KPI. INP is also important to regularly monitor because it is part of Google's Core Web Vitals and may impact SEO performance.

- **Does it describe the user experience?** INP describes the experience visitors have interacting with the page more effectively than any other metric discussed in this book. Visitors will have a poor experience and grow frustrated if it takes a long time to see a response after interacting with an element on the page. INP also measures many different types of interactions, from simple interactions, like clicking links or buttons, to more involved interactions, like engaging with shopping carts or search forms. As a result, INP is a useful metric describing the user experience on many different types of websites.

- **How easy is it to improve?** Improvements depend on the stage of the interaction process with issues. Input Delay is harder to improve because it requires optimizing other tasks that slow the browser's ability to respond to the interaction. Improving Processing Time and Presentation Delay requires getting deeper into the webpage's code, especially JavaScript code, to understand why the page responds slowly to a visitor's interaction. Also, improving INP may require making some difficult trade-offs. Some features may need to be removed from the event handler code. Those removals could improve INP while taking away features visitors preferred, like more complex animations, or taking away features that were helpful for the business, like tracking scripts.

- **How impactful are improvements?** Although INP improvements can have positive impacts on user experience and website conversion rates, improvements in INP typically do not improve other speed metrics. There are exceptions. For example, improvements in INP may reduce main thread activity and can improve Total Blocking Time. INP has little impact on other speed metrics because it is a late-stage metric. By the time INP is being measured and visitors are interacting, the events measured by other speed metrics have already occurred because most of the website has finished loading.

CHAPTER 11

Conclusion: Choosing Website Speed Metrics

There are many different metrics that can be used to measure a website's speed. This can make reviewing speed reports seem overwhelming or challenging. It does need to be. To make the metrics more meaningful, remember where each metric fits in the overall website loading process. These metrics describe how the website loads, starting with the visitor's initial connection all the way through to their final interaction with a website.

When reviewing speed reports, group the metrics by the major loading stages and review the metrics for each stage in the order they occur. As summarized in Figure 11-1, the major loading stages are as follows:

- **Initial connection:** To begin, check the page's Time to First Byte. If it is slow, there are problems in the initial stages of loading the website. If the initial stages are slow, all other metrics will be slower. To identify where problems exist in the initial stages, measure the different components of Time to First Byte, including DNS Lookup Time. Improve the performance of the initial stages before addressing any of the later stages.

- **Displaying the page:** Once the initial stages load within an acceptable amount of time, review metrics related to the middle of the website loading process. This is the critical rendering path. To measure its speed, evaluate DOMContentLoaded time, Total Resources, Transfer Size, and First Contentful Paint. Problems with these metrics indicate delays in how quickly visitors can see and interact with the webpage. If there are problems in the middle stages of loading the website, fix those before addressing other, later-stage speed issues.

- **Completing the website load:** If the initial and middle stages are within acceptable levels, then measure the final stages of loading the website. There are different ways of measuring these final stages. Time to Interactive measures when visitors can begin interacting with the webpage and Total Blocking Time helps explain why Time to Interactive may be delayed. Speed Index measures how quickly visitors can see the page. Onload or Fully Loaded Time report when all resources have loaded.

- **User experience (Core Web Vitals):** Once those metrics describing the final loading stages are within acceptable levels, focus on metrics that describe the user experience. These are Google's Core Web Vitals metrics. Largest Contentful Paint measures when the browser paints the largest item in the first viewport, which is often the webpage's main content. Cumulative Layout Shift measures if layout shifts are creating a poor experience for visitors. Interaction to Next Paint measures how quickly the webpage responds to visitor interactions.

For additional help deciding when to use each metric and keeping track of what each metric measures, Appendix A provides a recap of each metric. This also includes a recap of each metric's benchmark times.

Figure 11-1. *Metrics Timeline – measure the major stages of the website load*

Summary

These recommendations are only a starting point. Every website is unique. The exact combination of metrics to regularly monitor and include in reports will change for every website. To find the most appropriate metrics to measure, choose the metrics that relate the most to the business's goal and best describe that website's user experience. As well, select the metrics that can be improved and, if improved, will positively impact the website's performance – there is no point regularly tracking metrics that cannot be improved due to entrenched technical issues or metrics that, if improved, would make little difference.

Monitor those chosen metrics regularly to understand how speed changes over time, especially as speed changes in response to speed optimization projects and other website updates. To help monitor those metrics, find the most appropriate speed tools. Some companies will find value investing in multiple tools, while other companies will find sufficient value in the free tools available.

Regardless of what metrics or tools are used, the most important thing is to measure at least some aspect of the website's speed. Doing so clarifies why the website loads slowly and identifies opportunities to make the website load faster.

APPENDIX A

Metrics Recap

Regular Monitoring

Metrics to monitor on a continuous basis to spot any concerning trends or new problems.

Metric	What It Measures	Target*	Median*	Best For
Time to First Byte (TTFB)	When the server returns the first byte of data to the browser	Under 800 milliseconds	n/a	Regular monitoring
Total Requests	Total number of files requested	n/a	Mobile: 67 filesDesktop: 71 files	Regular monitoring
Transfer Size	Total bytes transferred from the server to the browser	n/a	Mobile: 2.2 MBDesktop: 2.4 MB	Regular monitoring
Total Blocking Time (TBT)	How long the browser was blocked by long tasks and unable to respond	Under 200 milliseconds	n/a	Regular monitoring

© Matthew Edgar 2024
M. Edgar, *Speed Metrics Guide*, https://doi.org/10.1007/979-8-8688-0155-6

Core Web Vitals – SEO and UX

Important metrics to monitor to understand website user experience and watch for SEO impacts. These can also be helpful KPIs given their impact on SEO.

Metric	What It Measures	Target*	Median*	Best For
Largest Contentful Paint (LCP)	When the browser paints the largest content element in the first viewport	Under 2.5 seconds	n/a	Core Web VitalsRegular monitoring Speed KPI
Interaction to Next Paint (INP)	How quickly the webpage shows a visual response to an interaction	Under 200 milliseconds	n/a	Core Web VitalsRegular monitoring Speed KPI
Cumulative Layout Shift (CLS)	How visually stable elements are on a webpage	Under 0.1	n/a	Core Web VitalsRegular monitoring

Speed KPIs

Metrics to consider including in reports for stakeholders about website speed.

Metric	What It Measures	Target*	Median*	Best For
First Contentful Paint (FCP)	When the browser paints the first content	Under 1.8 seconds	Mobile: 3.8 secondsDesktop: 2.3 seconds	Regular monitoring Speed KPI
Time to Interactive (TTI)	When the website can reliably respond to interactions	Under 3.8 seconds	Mobile: 14.3 secondsDesktop: 4.2 seconds	Speed KPI
Speed Index	How quickly the webpage became visually complete	Under 3.4 seconds	Mobile: 6.5 secondsDesktop: 4.3 seconds	Speed KPIRegular monitoring

Deeper Diagnostic

Metrics that help diagnose deeper problems on the website if issues arise in regularly monitored metrics or speed KPIs.

Metric	What It Measures	Target*	Median*	Best For
DNS Lookup Time	How long the browser takes to retrieve the IP address	20–120 milliseconds	n/a	Deeper diagnostic
DomContent Loaded (DCL) Time	When the browser fully parses the webpage's HTML	n/a	Mobile: 6.2 secondsDesktop: 3.1 seconds	Deeper diagnostic

For General Communication

Metrics that may be useful when discussing speed with a broader audience.

Metric	What It Measures	Target*	Median*	Best For
Onload Time	When the browser loads all dependent resources	n/a	Mobile: 10.6 secondsDesktop: 6.5 seconds	As needed when communicating total speed
Fully Loaded Time	Onload Time + some amount of network idle time	n/a	n/a	As needed when communicating total speed

Median and benchmark data sources provided in each chapter.

APPENDIX B

PageSpeed Insights

One of the most recommended speed monitoring tools is PageSpeed Insights offered by Google (`https://pagespeed.web.dev/`). This tool can measure many of the metrics discussed in this book. While a helpful tool, it was not included in individual chapters to avoid redundancy. This appendix provides a brief overview of what PageSpeed Insights offers.

The most interesting aspect of PageSpeed Insights is that the tool's reports include two types of data, field data and lab data. Lab data simulates a load of the website and evaluates speed based on that simulation. Field data reports how real-world visitors experienced speed during their visit to the website. Data is available for mobile and desktop devices. PageSpeed Insights also provides opportunities and diagnostic information to help improve website speed.

Field Data

Field data is sourced from Chrome's User Experience (CrUX) dataset and represents data from website visitors using Google Chrome over the last 28 days. Field data is only available for pages with enough real-world data, so pages with low visit counts will not have data available. Field data is also only available for pages that are publicly discoverable, which means the page can be indexed in search results and that the page does not return an

M. Edgar, *Speed Metrics Guide*, https://doi.org/10.1007/979-8-8688-0155-6

error message or redirect. This data can be viewed in the "Discover what your real users are experiencing" section for mobile or desktop devices. An example is shown in Figure B-1 with reports for the following metrics:

- Largest Contentful Paint (LCP)

- First Input Delay (FID)

- Cumulative Layout Shift (CLS)

- First Contentful Paint (FCP)

- Interaction to Next Paint (INP)

- Time to First Byte (TTFB)

Figure B-1. *Field data in PageSpeed Insights*

The number above the bar represents the 75th percentile for the values in the CrUX dataset. For example, in Figure B-1, LCP is 2.1 seconds. That means 75% of visitors experienced an LCP of 2.1 seconds or lower.

The more important information is in the table shown after clicking "Expand View" (that link is to the upper right of the metrics). This shows the distribution of observed values for real-world visitors. This data is also used to determine the length of each segment of the horizontal bar. Figure B-2 shows an expanded view of TTFB. The first row of data shows that 50% of visitors experienced a Good TTFB under 800 milliseconds. Because of this, the first part of the bar, in green, is 50% of the bar length. The second row of data and the middle part of the bar, in yellow, shows that 34% of visitors experienced a TTFB that Needs Improvement between 800 milliseconds and 1800 milliseconds. The final part of the bar, in red, and the last row of data shows 15% of visitors experienced a Poor TTFB greater than 1800 milliseconds.

Figure B-2. Expand View showing details of how visitors experienced TTFB

Lab Data

Because lab data is based on a simulated load of the website, it will be available for all pages tested, regardless of how much real-world data exists and regardless of if the page can be indexed in search results. This makes lab data useful for evaluating speed on new pages or pages currently in development. Lab data is available in the "Diagnose performance issues" section of the report for mobile or desktop devices. An example is shown in Figure B-3. Lab data provides data about these metrics:

- First Contentful Paint (FCP)

- Total Blocking Time (TBT)

- Speed Index

- Largest Contentful Paint (LCP)

- Cumulative Layout Shift (CLS)

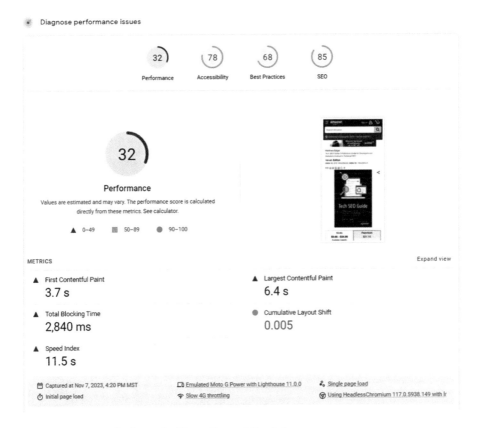

Figure B-3. *Lab data in PageSpeed Insights*

Lab data also includes a Performance score, which is 32 in Figure B-3. The Performance score is not a direct measurement of a website's speed. Instead, this is a weighted average of some of the speed metrics evaluated in this data. The current weights are shown in Table B-1. Total Blocking Time will have the greatest impact on the score, while First Contentful Paint and Speed Index will have the least impact on the score.

Table B-1. *Performance Score Weighted Averages, Lighthouse 10*

Audit	Weight
First Contentful Paint	10%
Speed Index	10%
Largest Contentful Paint	25%
Total Blocking Time	30%
Cumulative Layout Shift	25%

The Performance score can be a quick indication of a website's speed, at least as it relates to the five metrics factored into the average. However, because it is a weighted average, the Performance score misses many of the details about each of these metrics. Any serious evaluation of the website's speed should review individual speed metrics instead of the Performance score. Any speed optimization projects should be evaluated against changes in individual metrics instead of changes in the Performance score.

Importantly, Google does not use the Performance score to evaluate the SEO impacts of Core Web Vitals. Instead, Google uses the observed metric values for LCP, INP, and CLS. Importantly, INP is not included within the Performance score because it cannot be evaluated as part of Lab data. INP can only be evaluated for real-word visitors and, therefore, is only available within Field data.

Opportunities and Diagnostics

PageSpeed Insights also provides opportunities and diagnostics information at the end of the report. This can be useful to understand what problems exist on the website and what could be improved. For example, in Figure B-4, the "Opportunities" section shows that unused JavaScript is adding 5.29 seconds to the entire website load. The "Diagnostics" section reports that main-thread work could be minimized by up to 32 seconds. This section will also include details about each of the Core Web Vitals metrics. For example, Figure B-5 shows detailed information about which elements are shifting and by how much. This information can be filtered to specific metrics using the filters to the upper right ("Show audits relevant to:").

It is important to note that the opportunities and diagnostic information is only a suggestion. While these are often helpful ways to improve website speed, there are other options. Only use these as a guide, not as the definitive list of items to improve on the website.

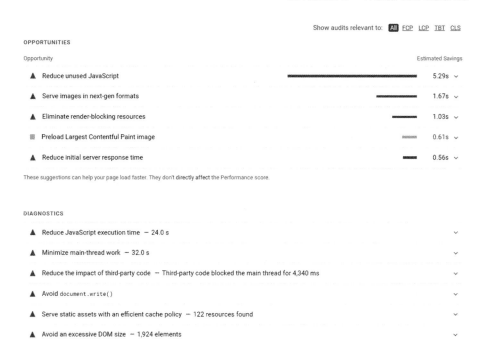

Figure B-4. *Opportunities and Diagnostics in PageSpeed Insights*

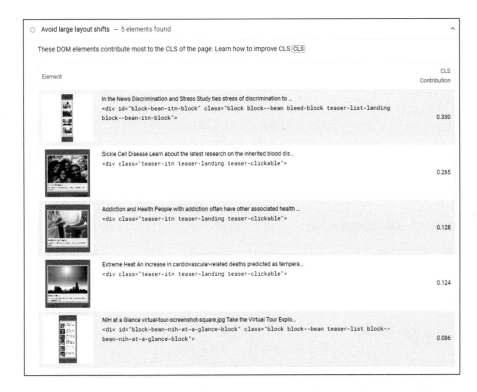

Figure B-5. *PageSpeed Insights Diagnostics showing layout shifts*

APPENDIX C

References and Additional Information

Chapter 1

"DNS Providers List." DNSPerf. PerfOps. Accessed November 3, 2023. `www.dnsperf.com/dns-providers-list`.

Jackson, Brian. 2017. "8 Tips on How to Reduce DNS Lookups and Speed Them Up." Kinsta. August 21, 2017. `https://kinsta.com/blog/reduce-dns-lookups/`.

Levine, Carl. 2016. "Decoding DIG Output." NS1. An IBM Company. July 13, 2016. `https://ns1.com/blog/decoding-dig-output`.

"Performance Benefits | Public DNS." 2018. Google Developers. September 4, 2018. `https://developers.google.com/speed/public-dns/docs/performance`.

Pramatarov, Martin. 2023. "What Is Authoritative DNS Server?" ClouDNS. April 19, 2023. `www.cloudns.net/blog/authoritative-dns-server/`.

"Using DNS-Prefetch." 2023. MDN Web Docs. July 4, 2023. `https://developer.mozilla.org/en-US/docs/Web/Performance/dns-prefetch`.

"What Is DNS Lookup Time & How to Reduce It?" 2023. Sematext. September 10, 2023. `https://sematext.com/glossary/dns-lookup-time/`.

"What Is DNS? How DNS Works." Cloudflare. `www.cloudflare.com/learning/dns/what-is-dns/`.

"What Is TTL (and How Do You Choose the Right One)?" 2022. Kinsta. October 28, 2022. `https://kinsta.com/knowledgebase/what-is-ttl/`.

Chapter 2

"A Typical HTTP Session." 2023. MDN Web Docs. April 10, 2023. `https://developer.mozilla.org/en-US/docs/Web/HTTP/Session`.

"About PageSpeed Insights." PageSpeed Insights. Google Developers. May 10, 2023. `https://developers.google.com/speed/docs/insights/v5/about`.
See "Assessing quality of experiences" section.

"How an SSL Connection Is Established."
IBM. November 2, 2022. www.ibm.com/docs/en/
cics-tg-zos/9.3.0?topic=ssl-how-connection-
is-established.

Marsh, Sam, Achiel van der Mandele, and Shih-
Chiang Chien. 2023. "Are You Measuring What
Matters? A Fresh Look at Time to First Byte." The
Cloudflare Blog. Cloudflare. June 20, 2023. https://
blog.cloudflare.com/ttfb-is-not-what-it-
used-to-be/.

"Report: CrUX." 2023. HTTP Archive. September 1,
2023. https://httparchive.org/reports/chrome-
ux-report#cruxFastTtfb.

"TCP 3-Way Handshake Process." GeeksforGeeks.
October 26, 2021. www.geeksforgeeks.org/tcp-3-
way-handshake-process/.

Wagner, Jeremy, and Barry Pollard. 2021. "Time
to First Byte (TTFB)." Web.dev. October 26, 2021.
https://web.dev/articles/ttfb.

"What Happens in a TLS Handshake? | SSL
Handshake." Cloudflare. Accessed September 15,
2023. www.cloudflare.com/learning/ssl/what-
happens-in-a-tls-handshake/.

Chapter 3

"Avoid an Excessive DOM Size." 2019. Chrome for Developers. Google for Developers. May 2, 2019, updated October 4, 2019. `https://developer.chrome.com/en/docs/lighthouse/performance/dom-size/#how-the-lighthouse-dom-size-audit-fails`.

"DOMContentLoaded Event." 2023. MDN Web Docs. August 4, 2023. `https://developer.mozilla.org/en-US/docs/Web/API/Document/DOMContentLoaded_event`.

Grigorik, Ilya. 2018. "Render-Tree Construction, Layout, and Paint." Web.dev. March 31, 2014. `https://web.dev/articles/critical-rendering-path/render-tree-construction`.

"Introduction to the DOM." 2023. MDN Web Docs. May 20, 2023. `https://developer.mozilla.org/en-US/docs/Web/API/Document_Object_Model/Introduction`.

Mihajlija, Milica. 2022. "Efficiently Load Third-Party JavaScript." Web.dev. August 14, 2019. `https://web.dev/articles/efficiently-load-third-party-javascript`.

"Report: Loading Speed." HTTP Archive. October 1, 2023. `https://httparchive.org/reports/loading-speed#dcl`.

Vernon, Timothy. 2020. "Improve Site Performance by Inlining Your CSS." LogRocket Blog. June 4, 2020. `https://blog.logrocket.com/improve-site-performance-inlining-css/`.

Wagner, Jeremy. 2023. "How Large DOM Sizes Affect Interactivity, and What You Can Do about It." Web. dev. May 9, 2023. `https://web.dev/articles/dom-size-and-interactivity`.

Yordanov, Evgeni. 2023. "Critical CSS: How to Boost Your Website's Speed and UX (Fix Render-Blocking CSS)." NitroPack. May 4, 2023. `https://nitropack.io/blog/post/critical-css`.

Chapter 4

"AVIF Image Format." Can I Use. Accessed November 13, 2023. `https://caniuse.com/avif`.

"Compression Techniques." 2023. WebP. Google Developers. September 14, 2023. `https://developers.google.com/speed/webp/docs/compression`.

Djirdeh, Houssein, and Jeremy Wagner. 2018. "Replace Animated GIFs with Video for Faster Page Loads." Web.dev. November 5, 2018. `https://web.dev/articles/replace-gifs-with-videos`.

"Domain Sharding." 2023. MDN Web Docs. June 8, 2023. `https://developer.mozilla.org/en-US/docs/Glossary/Domain_sharding`.

Evans, Cal. 2022. "The Difference between Brotli and GZIP Compression Algorithms to Speed up Your Site." SiteGround Blog. SiteGround Web Hosting. February 9, 2022. `www.siteground.com/blog/brotli-vs-gzip-compression/`.

Grigonis, Hillary K and Anita George. 2023. "JPEG vs. PNG: When and Why to Use One Format over the Other." Digital Trends. October 29, 2023. `www.digitaltrends.com/computing/jpeg-vs-png/`.

Hempenius, Katie, and Barry Pollard. 2021. "Best Practices for Fonts." Web.dev. October 4, 2022. `https://web.dev/articles/font-best-practices`.

Meenan, Patrick. 2015. "Resource Fetch Prioritization and Scheduling in Chrome." August 5, 2015, updated November 23, 2023. Retrieved from `https://docs.google.com/document/d/1bCDuq9H1ih9iNjgzyALOgpwNFiEP4TZS-YLRp_RuMlc/`. Unpublished manuscript.

Nanwani, Rahul. 2016. "JPEG vs PNG vs GIF - Which Image Format to Use and When?" ImageKit.io. November 14, 2016. `https://blog.imagekit.io/jpeg-vs-png-vs-gif-which-image-format-to-use-and-when-c8913ae3e01d`.

Osmani, Addy, Leena Sohoni, Patrick Meenan, and Barry Pollard. 2023. "Optimizing Resource Loading with the Fetch Priority API." Web.dev. November 14, 2023. `https://web.dev/articles/fetch-priority`.

Pollard, Barry. 2019. HTTP/2 in Action. Shelter Island, NY: Manning.
See Chapter 4, "HTTP/2 Protocol Basics".

Rajora, Harish. 2020. "AVIF Image Format - the Next-Gen Compression Codec." LambdaTest. October 19, 2020. www.lambdatest.com/blog/avif-image-format/.

Ravoof, Salman. 2023. "Brotli Compression: A Fast Alternative to GZIP Compression." Kinsta. June 19, 2023. https://kinsta.com/blog/brotli-compression/.

Rehman, Abdul. 2023. "Brotli vs. GZIP: A Comprehensive Comparison of Compression Algorithms." Cloudways. June 14, 2023. www.cloudways.com/blog/brotli-vs-gzip/.

"Report: Page Weight." HTTP Archive. October 1, 2023. https://httparchive.org/reports/page-weight.

"Should I Combine CSS/JS Files on My Website?" 2022. GTmetrix. March 17, 2022. https://gtmetrix.com/blog/should-i-combine-css-js-files-on-my-website/.

"Usage Statistics of Compression for Websites." 2023. W3Techs. Q-Success. November 20, 2023. https://w3techs.com/technologies/details/ce-compression.

Chapter 5

Bece, Adrian. 2020. "How to Load Fonts in a Way That Fights FOUT and Makes Lighthouse Happy." CSS-Tricks. Digital Ocean. November 24, 2020, updated December 6, 2020. `https://css-tricks.com/how-to-load-fonts-in-a-way-that-fights-fout-and-makes-lighthouse-happy/`.

"Critical Rendering Path." 2023. MDN Web Docs. July 4, 2023. `https://developer.mozilla.org/en-US/docs/Web/Performance/Critical_rendering_path`

Daggett, John, Myles C. Maxfield, and Chris Lilley, eds. 2021. "CSS Fonts Module Level 4." World Wide Web Consortium. December 21, 2021. `www.w3.org/TR/css-fonts-4/#font-display-desc`.

Dodson, Rob. 2016. "Controlling Font Performance with Font-Display." Chrome for Developers. Google for Developers. January 31, 2016. `https://developer.chrome.com/blog/font-display/`.

"Ensure Text Remains Visible during Webfont Load." 2019. Chrome for Developers. Google for Developers. May 2, 2019, updated April 29, 2020. `https://developer.chrome.com/docs/lighthouse/performance/font-display/`.

"First Contentful Paint." 2019. Chrome for Developers. Google for Developers. May 2, 2019, updated June 4, 2021. `https://developer.chrome.com/en/docs/lighthouse/performance/first-contentful-paint/#how-lighthouse-determines-your-fcp-score`.

"Font-Display – CSS: Cascading Style Sheets." 2023. MDN Web Docs. July 7, 2023. `https://developer.mozilla.org/en-US/docs/Web/CSS/@font-face/font-display`.

Frey, Simon. 2022. "Load Time vs Render Time. Find out How These Metrics Affect Your Website." Blog by Simon Frey. March 11, 2022. `https://simon-frey.com/blog/load-time-vs-render-time-find-out-how-these-metrics-affect-your-website/`.

Graham, Geoff. 2017. "Font-Display." CSS-Tricks. Digital Ocean. April 17, 2017, updated March 25, 2020. `https://css-tricks.com/almanac/properties/f/font-display/`.

Kaleev, Niko. 2023. "Critical Rendering Path: What It Is and How to Optimize It." NitroPack. April 20, 2023. `https://nitropack.io/blog/post/critical-rendering-path-optimization`.

"Lazy Loading Via Attribute for Images & Iframes" Can I Use. Accessed November 20, 2023. `https://caniuse.com/loading-lazy-attr`.

Osmani, Addy. 2023. "It's Time to Lazy-Load Offscreen Iframes!" Web.dev. October 11, 2023. `https://web.dev/articles/iframe-lazy-loading`.

Osmani, Addy, Houssein Djirdeh, Mathias Bynens, and Barry Pollard. 2023. "Browser-Level Image Lazy-Loading for the Web." Web.dev. June 2, 2023. `https://web.dev/articles/browser-level-image-lazy-loading`.

"Report: Loading Speed." HTTP Archive. October 1, 2023. https://httparchive.org/reports/loading-speed#fcp.

Schapira, Boris. 2019. "First Contentful Paint (FCP), Start Render, First Paint. How to Properly Measure the Beginning of Page Rendering?" Dareboost Blog. September 10, 2019. https://blog.dareboost.com/en/2019/09/first-contentful-paint-fcp/.

Chapter 6

Basques, Kayce, and Sofia Emelianova. 2017. "Performance Features Reference." Chrome for Developers. Google for Developers. May 8, 2017. https://developer.chrome.com/docs/devtools/performance/reference/.

"Measure and Optimize Total Blocking Time (TBT)." 2023. DebugBear. June 18, 2023. www.debugbear.com/docs/metrics/total-blocking-time.

"Minimize Main-Thread Work." GTmetrix. https://gtmetrix.com/minimize-main-thread-work.html.

"Report: Loading Speed." HTTP Archive. January 1, 2024. https://httparchive.org/reports/loading-speed#ttci.

Paralkar, Keyur. 2022. "How Web Workers Work in JavaScript – with a Practical JS Example." FreeCodeCamp. January 4, 2022. www.freecodecamp.org/news/how-webworkers-work-in-javascript-with-example/.

Souders, Steve. 2019. "Measuring Jank and UX." SpeedCurve. May 1, 2019. www.speedcurve.com/blog/measuring-jank-and-ux/.

Surma. 2019. "Use Web Workers to Run JavaScript off the Browser's Main Thread." Web.dev. December 5, 2019. https://web.dev/articles/off-main-thread.

"Time to Interactive." 2019. Chrome for Developers. Google for Developers. May 2, 2019, updated June 4, 2021. https://developer.chrome.com/docs/lighthouse/performance/interactive/#how-lighthouse-determines-your-tti-score.

"Time to Interactive." 2023. DebugBear. May 17, 2023. www.debugbear.com/docs/metrics/time-to-interactive.

"Total Blocking Time." GTmetrix. https://gtmetrix.com/total-blocking-time.html.

"Total Blocking Time." Chrome Developers. October 9, 2019, updated June 4, 2021. https://developer.chrome.com/docs/lighthouse/performance/lighthouse-total-blocking-time/#how-lighthouse-determines-your-tbt-score.

"Using Web Workers." 2023. MDN Web Docs. October 12, 2023. https://developer.mozilla.org/en-US/docs/Web/API/Web_Workers_API/Using_web_workers.

Wagner, Jeremy, and Paul Lewis. 2015. "Avoid Large, Complex Layouts and Layout Thrashing." Web. dev. March 20, 2015. `https://web.dev/articles/avoid-large-complex-layouts-and-layout-thrashing`.

Walton, Philip. 2019. "Time to Interactive (TTI)." Web.dev. November 7, 2019. `https://web.dev/articles/tti`.

Walton, Phillip. 2019. "Total Blocking Time (TBT)." Web.dev. November 7, 2019. `https://web.dev/articles/tbt`.

Yordanov, Evgeni. 2022. "Time to Interactive (TTI): What Is It and How to Improve It." Nitropack. December 23, 2022. `https://nitropack.io/blog/post/time-to-interactive-tti`.

Chapter 7

Babich, Nick. 2022. "Progress Indicators: 4 Common Styles." UX Planet. October 5, 2022. `https://uxplanet.org/progress-indicators-4-common-styles-91a12b86060c`.

Bakusevych, Taras. 2023. "Loading & Progress Indicators — UI Components Series." UX Collective. July 11, 2023. `https://uxdesign.cc/loading-progress-indicators-ui-components-series-f4b1fc35339a`.

"Browser Timings." 2020. GTmetrix. November 16, 2020. `https://gtmetrix.com/blog/browser-timings/`.

"Report: Loading Speed." HTTP Archive. October 1, 2023. `https://httparchive.org/reports/loading-speed`.

"Resource Usage Graphs Now Available." 2016. GTmetrix. November 3, 2016. `https://gtmetrix.com/blog/resource-usage-graphs-now-available/`.

"Speed Index." 2019. Chrome for Developers. Google for Developers. May 2, 2019, updated June 4, 2021. `https://developer.chrome.com/en/docs/lighthouse/performance/speed-index/#how-lighthouse-determines-your-speed-index-score`.

"Speed Index." WebPageTest Documentation. WebPageTest. `https://docs.webpagetest.org/metrics/speedindex/`.

Tankala, Samhita. 2023. "Skeleton Screens 101." Nielsen Norman Group. June 4, 2023. `www.nngroup.com/articles/skeleton-screens/`.

"Window: Load Event - Web APIs." 2023. MDN Web Docs. August 4, 2023. `https://developer.mozilla.org/en-US/docs/Web/API/Window/load_event`.

Chapter 8

"A New Image Format for the Web." 2023.
WebP. Google for Developers. September 14, 2023.
`https://developers.google.com/speed/webp`.

"AVIF Image Format." Can I Use. Accessed
November 13, 2023, updated January 3, 2023.
`https://caniuse.com/avif`.

"AVIF vs. WebP: 4 Key Differences and How to
Choose." 2023. Cloudinary. July 14, 2023, updated
October 25, 2023. `https://cloudinary.com/
guides/image-formats/avif-vs-webp-4-key-
differences-and-how-to-choose`.

Edgar, Matthew. 2023. "View Viewport or Browser
Size in GA4." Matthew Edgar. Elementive. October 2,
2023. `www.matthewedgar.net/google-analytics-
viewport-or-browser-size/`.

Garcia, Manuel, Dikla Cohen, Patrícia Couto Neto,
and Rui Santos. 2022. "Luxury Retailer Farfetch Sees
Higher Conversion Rates for Better Core Web Vitals."
Web.dev. July 12, 2022. `https://web.dev/case-
studies/farfetch`.

"LargestContentfulPaint." 2023. MDN Web
Docs. February 20, 2023. `https://developer.
mozilla.org/en-US/docs/Web/API/
LargestContentfulPaint`.

LargestContentfulPaint API Project Contributors. "Largest Contentful Paint Explainer." Specification for the LargestContentfulPaint API. World Wide Web Consortium. https://github.com/w3c/largest-contentful-paint.

"LargestContentfulPaint: Size Property." 2023. MDN Web Docs. April 7, 2023. https://developer.mozilla.org/en-US/docs/Web/API/LargestContentfulPaint/size.

McQuade, Bryan. 2022. "Defining the Core Web Vitals Metrics Thresholds." Web.dev. July 18, 2022. https://web.dev/articles/defining-core-web-vitals-thresholds.

"Measure and Optimize Largest Contentful Paint (LCP)." 2023. DebugBear. October 8, 2023. www.debugbear.com/docs/metrics/largest-contentful-paint.

Osmani, Addy. 2021. "Using Modern Image Formats: AVIF and WebP." Smashing Magazine. September 29, 2021. www.smashingmagazine.com/2021/09/modern-image-formats-avif-webp/.

"Report: CrUX." 2023. HTTP Archive. October 1, 2023. https://httparchive.org/reports/chrome-ux-report#cruxFastLcp.

Schmitz, Justin. 2021. "What Color Bit Depth Does AVIF Support?" Avif.io. January 3, 2021. https://avif.io/blog/faq/avif-bitdepth/.

"Usage Statistics of Image File Formats for Websites."
2023. W3Techs. Q-Success. November 13, 2023.
`https://w3techs.com/technologies/overview/`
`image_format.`

Walton, Philip, and Barry Pollard. 2023. "Largest
Contentful Paint (LCP)." Web.dev. August 4, 2023.
`https://web.dev/articles/lcp.`

"WebP." Can I Use. Accessed November 13, 2023.
`https://caniuse.com/webp.`

Weiss, Yoav, and Nicolás Peña Moreno, eds. 2023.
"Largest Contentful Paint." World Wide Web
Consortium. September 6, 2023. `www.w3.org/TR/`
`largest-contentful-paint/.`

Chapter 9

Kobes, Steve, Nicolás Peña Moreno, and Emily
Hanley, eds. 2021. "Layout Instability API." Web
Incubator Community Group. World Wide Web
Consortium. December 20, 2021. `https://wicg.`
`github.io/layout-instability/.`

Layout Instability Specification Project Contributors.
2021. "Explainer: Layout Instability Metric." Web
Incubator Community Group. World Wide Web
Consortium. December 20, 2021. `https://github.`
`com/WICG/layout-instability.`

"Measure and Optimize Cumulative Layout Shift (CLS)." 2023. DebugBear. June 18, 2023. `www.debugbear.com/docs/metrics/cumulative-layout-shift`.

McQuade, Bryan. 2022. "Defining the Core Web Vitals Metrics Thresholds." Web.dev. July 18, 2022. `https://web.dev/articles/defining-core-web-vitals-thresholds`.

Mihajlija, Milica, and Philip Walton. 2023. "Cumulative Layout Shift (CLS)." Web.dev. April 12, 2023. `https://web.dev/articles/cls`.

"Minimize Layout Shift." 2023. Google Publisher Tag. Google for Developers. August 23, 2023. `https://developers.google.com/publisher-tag/guides/minimize-layout-shift`.

Pollard, Barry. 2021. "How to Fix Cumulative Layout Shift (CLS) Issues." Smashing Magazine. June 2, 2021. `www.smashingmagazine.com/2021/06/how-to-fix-cumulative-layout-shift-issues/`.

Pollard, Barry. 2022. "Setting Height and Width on Images Is Important Again." Smashing Magazine. January 11, 2022. `www.smashingmagazine.com/2020/03/setting-height-width-images-important-again/`.

"Report: CrUX." 2023. HTTP Archive. October 1, 2023. `https://httparchive.org/reports/chrome-ux-report#cruxSmallCls`.

Sullivan, Annie, and Hongbo Song. 2021. "Evolving the CLS Metric." Web.dev. April 7, 2021. `https://web.dev/articles/evolving-cls`.

Zeman, Mark. 2023. "Demystifying Cumulative Layout Shift with CLS Windows." SpeedCurve. August 1, 2023. `www.speedcurve.com/blog/cls-windows-core-web-vitals/`.

Chapter 10

Andrew, Rachel. 2020. "Why Are Some Animations Slow?" Web.dev. October 6, 2020. `https://web.dev/articles/animations-overview`.

"Animation Performance and Frame Rate." 2023. MDN Web Docs. July 4, 2023. `https://developer.mozilla.org/en-US/docs/Web/Performance/Animation_performance_and_frame_rate`.

"CSS and JavaScript Animation Performance." 2023. MDN Web Docs. July 17, 2023. `https://developer.mozilla.org/en-US/docs/Web/Performance/CSS_JavaScript_animation_performance`.

"Event Handling (Overview)." 2023. MDN Web Docs. July 19, 2023. `https://developer.mozilla.org/en-US/docs/Web/Events/Event_handlers`.

Kaleev, Niko. 2023. "How to Improve Interaction to Next Paint (INP)." NitroPack. October 6, 2023. `https://nitropack.io/blog/post/improve-interaction-to-next-paint-inp`.

"Measure and Optimize Interaction to Next Paint (INP)." 2023. DebugBear. September 25, 2023. `www.debugbear.com/docs/metrics/interaction-to-next-paint`.

"Report: CrUX." 2023. HTTP Archive. October 1, 2023. `https://httparchive.org/reports/chrome-ux-report#cruxFastInp`.

Wagner, Jeremy. 2023. "Interaction to Next Paint (INP)." Web.dev. June 28, 2023. `https://web.dev/articles/inp`.

Wagner, Jeremy, and Philip Walton. 2023. "Optimize Interaction to next Paint." Web.dev. May 19, 2023. `https://web.dev/articles/optimize-inp`.

Appendix B

"About PageSpeed Insights." 2023. PageSpeed Insights. Google for Developers. May 10, 2023. `https://developers.google.com/speed/docs/insights/v5/about`.

"Lighthouse Performance Scoring." 2019. Chrome for Developers. Google for Developers. September 19, 2019. `https://developer.chrome.com/docs/lighthouse/performance/performance-scoring/`.

Index

A, B, C

Cascading style sheets (CSS)
  critical rendering path, 74
  DOM file, 39
  requested file types, 54
  Total Requests/Transfer
    Size, 66, 67
Chrome's User Experience (CrUX),
  187, 188, 209
Content Delivery
  Network (CDN), 67
CSS Object Model (CSSOM), 74, 76
Cumulative Layout Shift (CLS)
  benchmarks, 166
  Chrome DevTools, 170–173
  cumulative shifting scores, 164
  expected *vs.* unexpected
    shifts, 159
  filmstrip view, 168, 170
  late-loading images/videos, 165
  late-running JavaScript files,
    174, 175
  layout shift
    distance fraction, 160, 161
    elements, 158
    expected shifts, 159
    impact fraction, 160–162
    transform property, 158
  meaning, 157, 165
  performance report/layout
    shifts, 171
  reserve space, 176–178
  SEO performance, 178
  session window, 162–164
  shifting element, 158
  slower speeds, 165
  unexpected shifting, 173
  viewport, 172
  WebPageTest, 166–170

D, E

DNS Lookup Time, 3
  benchmark test, 8
  connection view report, 11
  detailed table, 10
  DiG GUI, 12, 13
  DNS-prefetch/preconnect
    link, 15, 16
  domain connections, 10–12
  geographic location, 6
  IP address cache duration, 6
  map view, 9
  measuring process, 8
  process/numbers reference
    steps, 5

© Matthew Edgar 2024
M. Edgar, *Speed Metrics Guide*, https://doi.org/10.1007/979-8-8688-0155-6

U, V

W, X, Y, Z

Printed in the United States
by Baker & Taylor Publisher Services